365

DAYS OF

GRATITUDE

JOURNAL

Also by Mariëlle S. Smith

52 Weeks of Writing Author Journal and Planner, Vol. I: Get out of your own way and become the writer you're meant to be

52 Weeks of Writing Author Journal and Planner, Vol. II: Get out of your own way and become the writer you're meant to be

Get Out of Your Own Way: A 31-Day Tarot Challenge for Writers and Other Creatives
(also available in Spanish and Dutch)

Tarot for Creatives: 21 Tarot Spreads to (Re)Connect to Your Intuition and Ignite that Creative Spark
(also available in Spanish, French, and Dutch)

Fleshing Out the Narrative: A 31-Day Tarot and Journal Challenge for Writers

Set Yourself Up for Success: A 31-Day Tarot Challenge for Writers and Other Creatives

Seven Simple Spreads Book 1: Seven Simple Card Spreads to Unlock Your Creative Flow

Seven Simple Spreads Book 2: Seven Simple Card Spreads to Direct Your Creative Flow

Seven Simple Spreads Book 3: Seven Simple Card Spreads to Boost Your Confidence

Seven Simple Spreads Book 4: Seven Simple Card Spreads to Celebrate Your Creative Wins

Speak Your Truth: A 31-Day Tarot Challenge for Writers and Other Creatives

Step into Your Power: A 31-Day Tarot Challenge to Unleash Your Creative Potential

Co-written under the pen name Heather Maclee

Too Good to Be True?

Where There's a Will

There's a Way

365

DAYS OF GRATITUDE JOURNAL

Commit to the life-changing power of
gratitude by creating a sustainable practice

Mariëlle S. Smith

TO MUM

Introduction

Welcome to *365 Days of Gratitude*, a journal for those who want to create a sustainable gratitude practice. I'm so grateful that you're here.

Over the years, I've tested various ways of 'doing' gratitude journaling, keeping what served me and discarding what didn't. What you have in front of you right now is what I kept after all that trying.

Why gratitude?

I'm not here to sell you on gratitude. There are many articles and research papers I could be citing to convince you just how great practising gratitude is for you. I think you're already aware of that, though. Perhaps you've read some of those articles and papers or maybe you just know it somewhere deep down —or not so deep down.

I'm not hooked on gratitude because it works wonders on my blood pressure and promises to help me sleep better. Although it probably does that, too.

I'm hooked on gratitude because it enables me to perceive everything in life as magical again. I'm hooked because I'm not the same person I was since I started practising it. And because I slip and return to being that anxious, burned out, overachieving workaholic as soon as I stray from the gratitude path—which happens far more often than I care to admit.

Gratitude is a commitment for life. I created this journal to help you commit and turn your gratitude practice into a sustainable one.

Serendipity + structure = sustainability

Serendipity

My gratitude practice started almost three years ago. I had a job that drained me, was in a relationship that hadn't been working for quite some time, and my yoga practice didn't fulfil me the way it used to. I had picked up regular journaling a few months prior and—hoping it would help snap me out of whatever I was going through at the time—had also committed myself to a daily meditation practice.

About a week after I started my daily meditations, I ran into an old university buddy from the time I lived in Dublin. Over the years, my once cynical friend had developed a dedicated daily meditation and gratitude practice.

I had dabbled in gratitude journaling before but had never been able to stick with it. I thought it wasn't for me. Then again, I couldn't quite believe just how much my friend had changed since we met last... When he offered to share the prompts he used in his daily gratitude practice before we went our separate ways, I didn't hesitate.

Structure

During my original attempts at gratitude journaling, I simply tried to write down at least one thing that had made me grateful that day. For whatever reason, that didn't work for me. Those prompts my friend shared did work.

Now that I had specific questions to answer, writing down what I felt grateful for no longer felt forced. I wasn't staring at the page anymore, trying to figure out what to write about. It made it so much easier to return the next day, and the next. It also enabled me to compare my answers and track my progress, which kept me coming back for more.

Once I realised which of the prompts didn't work for me, I began to leave some out, modified others, and brought in new questions to answer, the final result of which I am now sharing with you.

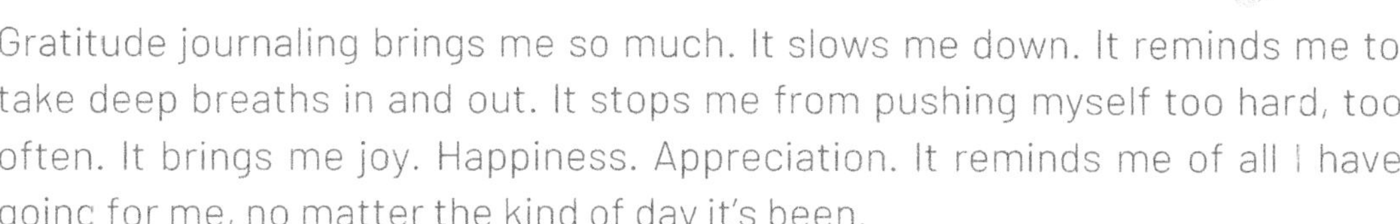

Sustainability

Gratitude journaling brings me so much. It slows me down. It reminds me to take deep breaths in and out. It stops me from pushing myself too hard, too often. It brings me joy. Happiness. Appreciation. It reminds me of all I have going for me, no matter the kind of day it's been.

It really has been the key I was looking and ready for when it showed up in my life.

But, even now, after years of practice, I have to consciously decide to do the work. That it came at the right time and with the structure I needed doesn't mean I don't get off track, especially when the going gets tough.

I used to become angry and utterly frustrated with myself when this happened, but now I simply sit myself down (read: force myself to take a break) and return to my practice. And because it's such a simple, structured practice, it's easier to pick up again than I often think.

Of course, some days or even weeks will be easier than others, but that's another thing gratitude journaling has brought me. No matter how far I stray, I am grateful for having something to return to. For all the days I ignore my practice, I'm grateful for all the days I do pick up my journal and let the miracle that is life unfold in front of me.

That attitude, that's what gratitude practice is all about for me. And I would never have developed it if it weren't for the prompts in this book. It is my hope that they will help you develop that same attitude so you can reap the same benefits.

Mariëlle

How to use 365 Days of Gratitude

This undated journal is set up as an evening journal, something you attend to when leaving the day behind. However, if you prefer to do your gratitude practice in the morning, just answer the prompts about the previous day instead. (I do so all the time.)

- Daily prompts

Three things I'm grateful for

Here, you get to write down the things you're grateful for, whether they are general or specific to that day. You can also mix it up and, for example, write down one thing you're grateful for in general and two things you're grateful for that happened in the past twenty-four hours.

I give today a

I rate my days anywhere between 1 and 10, but you might be more comfortable using a star system or rating your days from 1 to 5.

Something I want to remember about today

Anything in particular you want to remember about that day goes here. This could be anything, whether big or small.

Something I could have been more grateful for today

Here, you get to ponder something you could have been more grateful for that day. Perhaps something happened that you weren't grateful for at the time. Or maybe you took something for granted that you wish you hadn't. Whatever it is, here you get the chance to express gratitude for it after all.

My intention for tomorrow

No matter how the day went, there's always the next. Here, you can write down your intention for that next day. With what mindset do you want to tackle it? With what attitude towards yourself and others?

- Weekly & four-weekly prompts

Most weekly and four-weekly prompts are almost identical to the daily ones. However, instead of asking you to reflect on one day, you're asked to think back on the past week or four-week period as a whole.

Someone I could have felt more grateful for

Similar to the *Something I could have felt more grateful for* prompt, this prompt invites you to think of an individual, or individuals, who you could have been more grateful for. Did you have any encounters or conversations over the past week or four-week period that, in hindsight, you could have appreciated more?

Perhaps someone said 'No' to something and it turned out a big or small blessing. Maybe you had trouble feeling grateful for someone else's happiness or success. Whatever it was, here you get the chance to express gratitude for it after all.

- Quarterly prompts

Next to the ones you're already familiar with, the three-month checkpoint also includes prompts that invite you to pause a little longer and reflect a little deeper.

Looking back over the past three months, I am most grateful for

Here, I invite you to leaf through the past quarter. What do you notice about your previous entries and what, when looking back, are you the most grateful for?

The biggest lesson I learned over the past three months

What bigger lessons do your previous entries point towards? How can these be summed up best?

When looking back on how I've rated my weeks thus far, the numbers tell me

When comparing how you've rated the previous weeks, have you been doing better than you thought? Worse? Or have you been doing exactly like you thought you were? Have you been honest with your ratings or have you been pushing it? Whatever comes up, write it down.

What/who have I been unable to feel grateful for during the past three months?

No matter how much gratitude you have practised over the past quarter, there might still be that one (or more) thing, event, person that you just haven't been able to feel any gratitude towards.

Here, I invite you to rephrase your thoughts anyway, even if you're not feeling it (yet). Writing it down might just shift something for you, even if it's minor. You don't have to start with your biggest struggle here. If this is particularly hard for you, pick whatever feels doable.

I've said it before, but I will say it again: practising gratitude truly is a commitment for life. I hope that the prompts discussed here will help you turn your practice into a habit you can't help but return to.

Life is a series of thousands of tiny miracles.
Notice them.

Roald Dahl

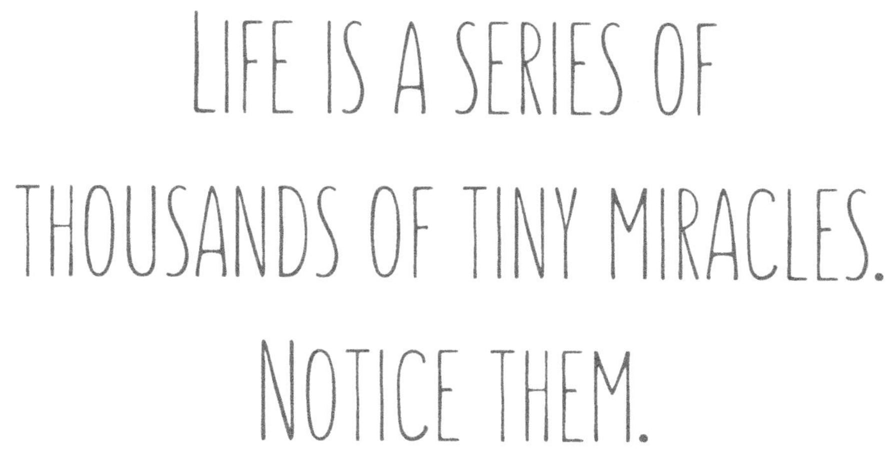

DAY 1

DAY   MONTH   YEAR

THREE THINGS I'M GRATEFUL FOR

I GIVE TODAY A   SOMETHING I WANT TO REMEMBER ABOUT TODAY

SOMETHING I COULD HAVE BEEN MORE GRATEFUL FOR TODAY   MY INTENTION FOR
TOMORROW

Day 2

Three things I'm grateful for

Something I want to remember about today

I give today a

My intention for
tomorrow

Something I could have been more grateful for today

DAY 3

DAY   MONTH   YEAR

THREE THINGS I'M GRATEFUL FOR

I GIVE TODAY A

SOMETHING I WANT TO REMEMBER ABOUT TODAY

SOMETHING I COULD HAVE BEEN MORE GRATEFUL FOR TODAY

MY INTENTION FOR TOMORROW

Day 4

Three things I'm grateful for

Something I want to remember about today

I give today a

My intention for
tomorrow

Something I could have been more grateful for today

DAY 5

DAY   MONTH   YEAR

THREE THINGS I'M GRATEFUL FOR

I GIVE TODAY A

SOMETHING I WANT TO REMEMBER ABOUT TODAY

SOMETHING I COULD HAVE BEEN MORE GRATEFUL FOR TODAY

MY INTENTION FOR TOMORROW

Day 6

Day   Month   Year

Three things I'm grateful for

Something I want to remember about today   I give today a

My intention for   Something I could have been more grateful for today
tomorrow

DAY 7

DAY   MONTH   YEAR

THREE THINGS I'M GRATEFUL FOR

I GIVE TODAY A   SOMETHING I WANT TO REMEMBER ABOUT TODAY

SOMETHING I COULD HAVE BEEN MORE GRATEFUL FOR TODAY   MY INTENTION FOR
TOMORROW

DAY 7

GRATITUDE IS A POWERFUL CATALYST FOR HAPPINESS.
IT'S THE SPARK THAT LIGHTS A FIRE OF JOY IN YOUR SOUL.
AMY COLLETTE

SOMETHING I COULD HAVE BEEN MORE GRATEFUL FOR THIS WEEK

I GIVE THIS WEEK A

SOMETHING I WANT TO REMEMBER ABOUT THIS WEEK

MY INTENTION FOR NEXT
WEEK

SOMEONE I COULD HAVE FELT MORE GRATEFUL FOR THIS WEEK

DAY 8

DAY   MONTH   YEAR

THREE THINGS I'M GRATEFUL FOR

I GIVE TODAY A

SOMETHING I WANT TO REMEMBER ABOUT TODAY

SOMETHING I COULD HAVE BEEN MORE GRATEFUL FOR TODAY

MY INTENTION FOR TOMORROW

Day 9

Day   Month   Year

Three things I'm grateful for

Something I want to remember about today

I give today a

My intention for
tomorrow

Something I could have been more grateful for today

DAY 10

THREE THINGS I'M GRATEFUL FOR

I GIVE TODAY A

SOMETHING I WANT TO REMEMBER ABOUT TODAY

SOMETHING I COULD HAVE BEEN MORE GRATEFUL FOR TODAY

MY INTENTION FOR TOMORROW

Day 11

Three things I'm grateful for

Something I want to remember about today

I give today a

My intention for
tomorrow

Something I could have been more grateful for today

DAY 12

DAY   MONTH   YEAR

THREE THINGS I'M GRATEFUL FOR

I GIVE TODAY A   SOMETHING I WANT TO REMEMBER ABOUT TODAY

SOMETHING I COULD HAVE BEEN MORE GRATEFUL FOR TODAY   MY INTENTION FOR TOMORROW

DAY 13

Day   Month   Year

Three things I'm grateful for

Something I want to remember about today

I give today a

My intention for tomorrow

Something I could have been more grateful for today

Day 14

Three things I'm grateful for

I give today a

Something I want to remember about today

Something I could have been more grateful for today

My intention for tomorrow

DAY 14

I WOULD MAINTAIN THAT THANKS ARE THE HIGHEST FORM OF THOUGHT, AND THAT GRATITUDE IS HAPPINESS DOUBLED BY WONDER.

Gilbert K. Chesterton

SOMETHING I COULD HAVE BEEN MORE GRATEFUL FOR THIS WEEK

I GIVE THIS WEEK A

SOMETHING I WANT TO REMEMBER ABOUT THIS WEEK

MY INTENTION FOR NEXT WEEK

SOMEONE I COULD HAVE FELT MORE GRATEFUL FOR THIS WEEK

DAY 15

DAY   MONTH   YEAR

THREE THINGS I'M GRATEFUL FOR

I GIVE TODAY A

SOMETHING I WANT TO REMEMBER ABOUT TODAY

SOMETHING I COULD HAVE BEEN MORE GRATEFUL FOR TODAY

MY INTENTION FOR TOMORROW

DAY 16

Three things I'm grateful for

Something I want to remember about today

I give today a

My intention for tomorrow

Something I could have been more grateful for today

Day 17

Three things I'm grateful for

I give today a

Something I want to remember about today

Something I could have been more grateful for today

My intention for tomorrow

DAY 18

DAY   MONTH   YEAR

THREE THINGS I'M GRATEFUL FOR

SOMETHING I WANT TO REMEMBER ABOUT TODAY

I GIVE TODAY A

MY INTENTION FOR
TOMORROW

SOMETHING I COULD HAVE BEEN MORE GRATEFUL FOR TODAY

DAY 19

THREE THINGS I'M GRATEFUL FOR

I GIVE TODAY A

SOMETHING I WANT TO REMEMBER ABOUT TODAY

SOMETHING I COULD HAVE BEEN MORE GRATEFUL FOR TODAY

MY INTENTION FOR
TOMORROW

DAY 20

THREE THINGS I'M GRATEFUL FOR

SOMETHING I WANT TO REMEMBER ABOUT TODAY

I GIVE TODAY A

MY INTENTION FOR
TOMORROW

SOMETHING I COULD HAVE BEEN MORE GRATEFUL FOR TODAY

DAY 21

Day   Month   Year

Three things I'm grateful for

I GIVE TODAY A   Something I want to remember about today

Something I could have been more grateful for today   My intention for
                                                             tomorrow

DAY 21

GRATITUDE UNLOCKS ALL THAT'S BLOCKING US FROM REALLY FEELING TRUTHFUL, REALLY FEELING AUTHENTIC AND VULNERABLE AND HAPPY.

GABRIELLE BERNSTEIN

SOMETHING I COULD HAVE BEEN MORE GRATEFUL FOR THIS WEEK

I GIVE THIS WEEK A

SOMETHING I WANT TO REMEMBER ABOUT THIS WEEK

MY INTENTION FOR NEXT WEEK

SOMEONE I COULD HAVE FELT MORE GRATEFUL FOR THIS WEEK

DAY 22

DAY   MONTH   YEAR

THREE THINGS I'M GRATEFUL FOR

I GIVE TODAY A   SOMETHING I WANT TO REMEMBER ABOUT TODAY

SOMETHING I COULD HAVE BEEN MORE GRATEFUL FOR TODAY   MY INTENTION FOR
                                                                       TOMORROW

Day 23

Day   Month   Year

Three things I'm grateful for

Something I want to remember about today

I give today a

My intention for
tomorrow

Something I could have been more grateful for today

Day 24

Day   Month   Year

Three things I'm grateful for

I give today a

Something I want to remember about today

Something I could have been more grateful for today

My intention for tomorrow

DAY 25

Day   Month   Year

Three things I'm grateful for

Something I want to remember about today   I give today a

My intention for
tomorrow   Something I could have been more grateful for today

DAY 26

THREE THINGS I'M GRATEFUL FOR

I GIVE TODAY A

SOMETHING I WANT TO REMEMBER ABOUT TODAY

SOMETHING I COULD HAVE BEEN MORE GRATEFUL FOR TODAY

MY INTENTION FOR TOMORROW

Day 27

Three things I'm grateful for

Something I want to remember about today

I give today a

My intention for
tomorrow

Something I could have been more grateful for today

DAY 28

Day   Month   Year

Three things I'm grateful for

I give today a

Something I want to remember about today

Something I could have been more grateful for today

My intention for tomorrow

DAY 28

GRATITUDE IS WHEN MEMORY IS STORED IN THE HEART AND NOT IN THE MIND.

LIONEL HAMPTON

SOMETHING I COULD HAVE BEEN MORE GRATEFUL FOR THESE PAST FOUR WEEKS

I GIVE THE PAST FOUR WEEKS A

SOMETHING I WANT TO REMEMBER ABOUT THE PAST FOUR WEEKS

MY INTENTION FOR THE NEXT FOUR WEEKS

SOMEONE I COULD HAVE FELT MORE GRATEFUL FOR THESE PAST FOUR WEEKS

DAY 29

THREE THINGS I'M GRATEFUL FOR

I GIVE TODAY A

SOMETHING I WANT TO REMEMBER ABOUT TODAY

SOMETHING I COULD HAVE BEEN MORE GRATEFUL FOR TODAY

MY INTENTION FOR
TOMORROW

DAY 30

Three things I'm grateful for

Something I want to remember about today

I give today a

My intention for tomorrow

Something I could have been more grateful for today

Day 31

Day   Month   Year

Three things I'm grateful for

I give today a

Something I want to remember about today

Something I could have been more grateful for today

My intention for tomorrow

Day 32

Day   Month   Year

Three things I'm grateful for

Something I want to remember about today

I give today a

My intention for
tomorrow

Something I could have been more grateful for today

DAY 33

THREE THINGS I'M GRATEFUL FOR

I GIVE TODAY A

SOMETHING I WANT TO REMEMBER ABOUT TODAY

SOMETHING I COULD HAVE BEEN MORE GRATEFUL FOR TODAY

MY INTENTION FOR TOMORROW

Day 34

Day   Month   Year

Three things I'm grateful for

Something I want to remember about today

I give today a

My intention for tomorrow

Something I could have been more grateful for today

Day 35

Three things I'm grateful for

I give today a

Something I want to remember about today

Something I could have been more grateful for today

My intention for tomorrow

DAY 35

Each day I am thankful for nights that turned into mornings,
friends that turned into family, dreams that turned into reality,
and likes that turned into love.

Unknown

Something I could have been more grateful for this week

I give this week a

Something I want to remember about this week

My intention for next
week

Someone I could have felt more grateful for this week

DAY 36

DAY   MONTH   YEAR

THREE THINGS I'M GRATEFUL FOR

I GIVE TODAY A

SOMETHING I WANT TO REMEMBER ABOUT TODAY

SOMETHING I COULD HAVE BEEN MORE GRATEFUL FOR TODAY

MY INTENTION FOR TOMORROW

Day 37

Day   Month   Year

Three things I'm grateful for

Something I want to remember about today

I give today a

My intention for tomorrow

Something I could have been more grateful for today

DAY 38

DAY   MONTH   YEAR

THREE THINGS I'M GRATEFUL FOR

I GIVE TODAY A

SOMETHING I WANT TO REMEMBER ABOUT TODAY

SOMETHING I COULD HAVE BEEN MORE GRATEFUL FOR TODAY

MY INTENTION FOR TOMORROW

Day 39

Three things I'm grateful for

Something I want to remember about today

I give today a

My intention for tomorrow

Something I could have been more grateful for today

DAY 40

THREE THINGS I'M GRATEFUL FOR

I GIVE TODAY A

SOMETHING I WANT TO REMEMBER ABOUT TODAY

SOMETHING I COULD HAVE BEEN MORE GRATEFUL FOR TODAY

MY INTENTION FOR TOMORROW

Day 41

Three things I'm grateful for

Something I want to remember about today

I give today a

My intention for tomorrow

Something I could have been more grateful for today

DAY 42

DAY   MONTH   YEAR

THREE THINGS I'M GRATEFUL FOR

I GIVE TODAY A   SOMETHING I WANT TO REMEMBER ABOUT TODAY

SOMETHING I COULD HAVE BEEN MORE GRATEFUL FOR TODAY   MY INTENTION FOR TOMORROW

DAY 42

GRATITUDE FOR THE PRESENT MOMENT AND THE FULLNESS OF LIFE NOW IS THE TRUE PROSPERITY.

ECKHART TOLLE

SOMETHING I COULD HAVE BEEN MORE GRATEFUL FOR THIS WEEK

I GIVE THIS WEEK A

SOMETHING I WANT TO REMEMBER ABOUT THIS WEEK

MY INTENTION FOR NEXT WEEK

SOMEONE I COULD HAVE FELT MORE GRATEFUL FOR THIS WEEK

DAY 43

DAY   MONTH   YEAR

THREE THINGS I'M GRATEFUL FOR

I GIVE TODAY A   SOMETHING I WANT TO REMEMBER ABOUT TODAY

SOMETHING I COULD HAVE BEEN MORE GRATEFUL FOR TODAY   MY INTENTION FOR TOMORROW

Day 44

Day   Month   Year

Three things I'm grateful for

Something I want to remember about today   I give today a

My intention for   Something I could have been more grateful for today
tomorrow

DAY 45

DAY   MONTH   YEAR

THREE THINGS I'M GRATEFUL FOR

I GIVE TODAY A

SOMETHING I WANT TO REMEMBER ABOUT TODAY

SOMETHING I COULD HAVE BEEN MORE GRATEFUL FOR TODAY

MY INTENTION FOR TOMORROW

Day 46

Day   Month   Year

Three things I'm grateful for

Something I want to remember about today

I give today a

My intention for
tomorrow

Something I could have been more grateful for today

DAY 47

DAY   MONTH   YEAR

THREE THINGS I'M GRATEFUL FOR

I GIVE TODAY A

SOMETHING I WANT TO REMEMBER ABOUT TODAY

SOMETHING I COULD HAVE BEEN MORE GRATEFUL FOR TODAY

MY INTENTION FOR
TOMORROW

DAY 48

DAY   MONTH   YEAR

THREE THINGS I'M GRATEFUL FOR

SOMETHING I WANT TO REMEMBER ABOUT TODAY

I GIVE TODAY A

MY INTENTION FOR
TOMORROW

SOMETHING I COULD HAVE BEEN MORE GRATEFUL FOR TODAY

DAY 49

DAY   MONTH   YEAR

THREE THINGS I'M GRATEFUL FOR

I GIVE TODAY A   SOMETHING I WANT TO REMEMBER ABOUT TODAY

SOMETHING I COULD HAVE BEEN MORE GRATEFUL FOR TODAY   MY INTENTION FOR
                                                             TOMORROW

DAY 49

Gratitude helps you to grow and expand; gratitude brings joy and laughter into your life and into the lives of all those around you.

Eileen Caddy

Something I could have been more grateful for this week

I give this week a

Something I want to remember about this week

My intention for next week

Someone I could have felt more grateful for this week

DAY 50

DAY   MONTH   YEAR

THREE THINGS I'M GRATEFUL FOR

I GIVE TODAY A   SOMETHING I WANT TO REMEMBER ABOUT TODAY

SOMETHING I COULD HAVE BEEN MORE GRATEFUL FOR TODAY   MY INTENTION FOR
TOMORROW

Day 51

Day   Month   Year

Three things I'm grateful for

Something I want to remember about today

I give today a

My intention for
tomorrow

Something I could have been more grateful for today

DAY 52

THREE THINGS I'M GRATEFUL FOR

I GIVE TODAY A

SOMETHING I WANT TO REMEMBER ABOUT TODAY

SOMETHING I COULD HAVE BEEN MORE GRATEFUL FOR TODAY

MY INTENTION FOR
TOMORROW

DAY 53

Day   Month   Year

Three things I'm grateful for

Something I want to remember about today   I give today a

My intention for   Something I could have been more grateful for today
tomorrow

DAY 54

THREE THINGS I'M GRATEFUL FOR

I GIVE TODAY A

SOMETHING I WANT TO REMEMBER ABOUT TODAY

SOMETHING I COULD HAVE BEEN MORE GRATEFUL FOR TODAY

MY INTENTION FOR TOMORROW

Day 55

Three things I'm grateful for

Something I want to remember about today

I give today a

My intention for
tomorrow

Something I could have been more grateful for today

DAY 56

DAY   MONTH   YEAR

THREE THINGS I'M GRATEFUL FOR

I GIVE TODAY A

SOMETHING I WANT TO REMEMBER ABOUT TODAY

SOMETHING I COULD HAVE BEEN MORE GRATEFUL FOR TODAY

MY INTENTION FOR TOMORROW

DAY 56

GRATITUDE OPENS THE DOOR TO THE POWER, THE WISDOM, THE CREATIVITY
OF THE UNIVERSE. YOU OPEN THE DOOR THROUGH GRATITUDE.

Deepak Chopra

SOMETHING I COULD HAVE BEEN MORE GRATEFUL FOR THESE
PAST FOUR WEEKS

I GIVE THE PAST FOUR WEEKS A

SOMETHING I WANT TO REMEMBER ABOUT THE PAST FOUR WEEKS

MY INTENTION FOR THE
NEXT FOUR WEEKS

SOMEONE I COULD HAVE FELT MORE GRATEFUL FOR THESE PAST
FOUR WEEKS

DAY 57

DAY   MONTH   YEAR

THREE THINGS I'M GRATEFUL FOR

I GIVE TODAY A   SOMETHING I WANT TO REMEMBER ABOUT TODAY

SOMETHING I COULD HAVE BEEN MORE GRATEFUL FOR TODAY   MY INTENTION FOR
                                                                       TOMORROW

DAY 58

THREE THINGS I'M GRATEFUL FOR

SOMETHING I WANT TO REMEMBER ABOUT TODAY

I GIVE TODAY A

MY INTENTION FOR
TOMORROW

SOMETHING I COULD HAVE BEEN MORE GRATEFUL FOR TODAY

Day 59

Day   Month   Year

Three things I'm grateful for

I give today a

Something I want to remember about today

Something I could have been more grateful for today

My intention for tomorrow

Day 60

Three things I'm grateful for

Something I want to remember about today

I give today a

My intention for
tomorrow

Something I could have been more grateful for today

DAY 61

DAY   MONTH   YEAR

THREE THINGS I'M GRATEFUL FOR

I GIVE TODAY A

SOMETHING I WANT TO REMEMBER ABOUT TODAY

SOMETHING I COULD HAVE BEEN MORE GRATEFUL FOR TODAY

MY INTENTION FOR TOMORROW

DAY 62

THREE THINGS I'M GRATEFUL FOR

SOMETHING I WANT TO REMEMBER ABOUT TODAY

I GIVE TODAY A

MY INTENTION FOR TOMORROW

SOMETHING I COULD HAVE BEEN MORE GRATEFUL FOR TODAY

DAY 63

DAY   MONTH   YEAR

THREE THINGS I'M GRATEFUL FOR

I GIVE TODAY A   SOMETHING I WANT TO REMEMBER ABOUT TODAY

SOMETHING I COULD HAVE BEEN MORE GRATEFUL FOR TODAY   MY INTENTION FOR TOMORROW

DAY 63

GRATITUDE IS AN ANTIDOTE TO NEGATIVE EMOTIONS, A NEUTRALIZER OF ENVY, HOSTILITY, WORRY, AND IRRITATION. IT IS SAVORING; IT IS NOT TAKING THINGS FOR GRANTED; IT IS PRESENT-ORIENTED.

Sonja Lyubomirsky

SOMETHING I COULD HAVE BEEN MORE GRATEFUL FOR THIS WEEK

I GIVE THIS WEEK A

SOMETHING I WANT TO REMEMBER ABOUT THIS WEEK

MY INTENTION FOR NEXT WEEK

SOMEONE I COULD HAVE FELT MORE GRATEFUL FOR THIS WEEK

DAY 64

DAY   MONTH   YEAR

THREE THINGS I'M GRATEFUL FOR

I GIVE TODAY A   SOMETHING I WANT TO REMEMBER ABOUT TODAY

SOMETHING I COULD HAVE BEEN MORE GRATEFUL FOR TODAY   MY INTENTION FOR TOMORROW

DAY 65

THREE THINGS I'M GRATEFUL FOR

SOMETHING I WANT TO REMEMBER ABOUT TODAY

I GIVE TODAY A

MY INTENTION FOR
TOMORROW

SOMETHING I COULD HAVE BEEN MORE GRATEFUL FOR TODAY

DAY 66

DAY MONTH YEAR

THREE THINGS I'M GRATEFUL FOR

I GIVE TODAY A

SOMETHING I WANT TO REMEMBER ABOUT TODAY

SOMETHING I COULD HAVE BEEN MORE GRATEFUL FOR TODAY

MY INTENTION FOR TOMORROW

Day 67

Day   Month   Year

Three things I'm grateful for

Something I want to remember about today   I give today a

My intention for   Something I could have been more grateful for today
tomorrow

DAY 68

THREE THINGS I'M GRATEFUL FOR

I GIVE TODAY A

SOMETHING I WANT TO REMEMBER ABOUT TODAY

SOMETHING I COULD HAVE BEEN MORE GRATEFUL FOR TODAY

MY INTENTION FOR TOMORROW

DAY 69

Three things I'm grateful for

Something I want to remember about today

I give today a

My intention for
tomorrow

Something I could have been more grateful for today

DAY 70

DAY   MONTH   YEAR

THREE THINGS I'M GRATEFUL FOR

I GIVE TODAY A   SOMETHING I WANT TO REMEMBER ABOUT TODAY

SOMETHING I COULD HAVE BEEN MORE GRATEFUL FOR TODAY   MY INTENTION FOR TOMORROW

DAY 70

START EACH DAY WITH A POSITIVE THOUGHT
AND A GRATEFUL HEART.

Roy T. Bennett

SOMETHING I COULD HAVE BEEN MORE GRATEFUL FOR THIS WEEK

I GIVE THIS WEEK A

SOMETHING I WANT TO REMEMBER ABOUT THIS WEEK

MY INTENTION FOR NEXT
WEEK

SOMEONE I COULD HAVE FELT MORE GRATEFUL FOR THIS WEEK

DAY 71

DAY   MONTH   YEAR

THREE THINGS I'M GRATEFUL FOR

I GIVE TODAY A   SOMETHING I WANT TO REMEMBER ABOUT TODAY

SOMETHING I COULD HAVE BEEN MORE GRATEFUL FOR TODAY   MY INTENTION FOR TOMORROW

Day 72

Month

Year

Three things I'm grateful for

Something I want to remember about today

I give today a

My intention for
tomorrow

Something I could have been more grateful for today

DAY 73

Day   Month   Year

Three things I'm grateful for

I give today a

Something I want to remember about today

Something I could have been more grateful for today

My intention for tomorrow

Day 74

Day   Month   Year

Three things I'm grateful for

Something I want to remember about today   I give today a

My intention for
tomorrow   Something I could have been more grateful for today

DAY 75

DAY   MONTH   YEAR

THREE THINGS I'M GRATEFUL FOR

I GIVE TODAY A

SOMETHING I WANT TO REMEMBER ABOUT TODAY

SOMETHING I COULD HAVE BEEN MORE GRATEFUL FOR TODAY

MY INTENTION FOR
TOMORROW

DAY 76

DAY   MONTH   YEAR

THREE THINGS I'M GRATEFUL FOR

SOMETHING I WANT TO REMEMBER ABOUT TODAY

I GIVE TODAY A

MY INTENTION FOR TOMORROW

SOMETHING I COULD HAVE BEEN MORE GRATEFUL FOR TODAY

Day 77

Day   Month   Year

Three things I'm grateful for

I give today a

Something I want to remember about today

Something I could have been more grateful for today

My intention for tomorrow

DAY 77

WHEN WE FOCUS ON OUR GRATITUDE, THE TIDE OF DISAPPOINTMENT GOES OUT AND THE TIDE OF LOVE RUSHES IN.

Kristin Armstrong

SOMETHING I COULD HAVE BEEN MORE GRATEFUL FOR THIS WEEK

I GIVE THIS WEEK A

SOMETHING I WANT TO REMEMBER ABOUT THIS WEEK

MY INTENTION FOR NEXT WEEK

SOMEONE I COULD HAVE FELT MORE GRATEFUL FOR THIS WEEK

DAY 78

DAY   MONTH   YEAR

THREE THINGS I'M GRATEFUL FOR

I GIVE TODAY A

SOMETHING I WANT TO REMEMBER ABOUT TODAY

SOMETHING I COULD HAVE BEEN MORE GRATEFUL FOR TODAY

MY INTENTION FOR TOMORROW

Day 79

Three things I'm grateful for

Something I want to remember about today   I give today a

My intention for   Something I could have been more grateful for today
tomorrow

DAY 80

DAY   MONTH   YEAR

THREE THINGS I'M GRATEFUL FOR

I GIVE TODAY A

SOMETHING I WANT TO REMEMBER ABOUT TODAY

SOMETHING I COULD HAVE BEEN MORE GRATEFUL FOR TODAY

MY INTENTION FOR
TOMORROW

Day 81

Day   Month   Year

Three things I'm grateful for

Something I want to remember about today

I give today a

My intention for
tomorrow

Something I could have been more grateful for today

DAY 82

DAY   MONTH   YEAR

THREE THINGS I'M GRATEFUL FOR

I GIVE TODAY A

SOMETHING I WANT TO REMEMBER ABOUT TODAY

SOMETHING I COULD HAVE BEEN MORE GRATEFUL FOR TODAY

MY INTENTION FOR
TOMORROW

DAY 83

Day   Month   Year

Three things I'm grateful for

Something I want to remember about today

I give today a

My intention for tomorrow

Something I could have been more grateful for today

DAY 84

DAY   MONTH   YEAR

THREE THINGS I'M GRATEFUL FOR

I GIVE TODAY A

SOMETHING I WANT TO REMEMBER ABOUT TODAY

SOMETHING I COULD HAVE BEEN MORE GRATEFUL FOR TODAY

MY INTENTION FOR TOMORROW

DAY 84

THERE IS A CALMNESS TO A LIFE LIVED IN GRATITUDE, A QUIET JOY.

Ralph H. Blum

SOMETHING I COULD HAVE BEEN MORE GRATEFUL FOR THESE PAST FOUR WEEKS

I GIVE THE PAST FOUR WEEKS A

SOMETHING I WANT TO REMEMBER ABOUT THE PAST FOUR WEEKS

MY INTENTION FOR THE NEXT FOUR WEEKS

SOMEONE I COULD HAVE FELT MORE GRATEFUL FOR THESE PAST FOUR WEEKS

DAY 85

DAY   MONTH   YEAR

THREE THINGS I'M GRATEFUL FOR

I GIVE TODAY A   SOMETHING I WANT TO REMEMBER ABOUT TODAY

SOMETHING I COULD HAVE BEEN MORE GRATEFUL FOR TODAY   MY INTENTION FOR TOMORROW

DAY 86

THREE THINGS I'M GRATEFUL FOR

SOMETHING I WANT TO REMEMBER ABOUT TODAY

I GIVE TODAY A

MY INTENTION FOR TOMORROW

SOMETHING I COULD HAVE BEEN MORE GRATEFUL FOR TODAY

DAY 87

DAY   MONTH   YEAR

THREE THINGS I'M GRATEFUL FOR

I GIVE TODAY A   SOMETHING I WANT TO REMEMBER ABOUT TODAY

SOMETHING I COULD HAVE BEEN MORE GRATEFUL FOR TODAY   MY INTENTION FOR
                                                           TOMORROW

Day 88

Day   Month   Year

Three things I'm grateful for

Something I want to remember about today   I give today a

My intention for   Something I could have been more grateful for today
tomorrow

DAY 89

DAY   MONTH   YEAR

THREE THINGS I'M GRATEFUL FOR

I GIVE TODAY A

SOMETHING I WANT TO REMEMBER ABOUT TODAY

SOMETHING I COULD HAVE BEEN MORE GRATEFUL FOR TODAY

MY INTENTION FOR TOMORROW

DAY 90

THREE THINGS I'M GRATEFUL FOR

SOMETHING I WANT TO REMEMBER ABOUT TODAY

I GIVE TODAY A

MY INTENTION FOR TOMORROW

SOMETHING I COULD HAVE BEEN MORE GRATEFUL FOR TODAY

DAY 91

DAY   MONTH   YEAR

THREE THINGS I'M GRATEFUL FOR

I GIVE TODAY A

SOMETHING I WANT TO REMEMBER ABOUT TODAY

SOMETHING I COULD HAVE BEEN MORE GRATEFUL FOR TODAY

MY INTENTION FOR TOMORROW

DAY 91

WHEN YOU LOVE WHAT YOU HAVE,
YOU HAVE EVERYTHING YOU NEED.

UNKNOWN

SOMETHING I COULD HAVE BEEN MORE GRATEFUL FOR THIS WEEK

I GIVE THIS WEEK A

SOMETHING I WANT TO REMEMBER ABOUT THIS WEEK

MY INTENTION FOR NEXT WEEK

SOMEONE I COULD HAVE FELT MORE GRATEFUL FOR THIS WEEK

3 MONTHS

Now you've come this far, it's time to look back.
Leaf through the past thirteen weeks and answer the following:

Something I want to remember about the past three months

Looking back over the past three months, I am most grateful for

The biggest lesson I learned over the past three months

Someone or something I could have felt more grateful for during the past three months

3 MONTHS

I GIVE THE PAST THREE MONTHS A

WHAT HAVE I BEEN UNABLE TO FEEL GRATEFUL FOR DURING THE PAST THREE MONTHS? CAN I REFORMULATE THAT THOUGHT ANYWAY?

I AM GRATEFUL...

WHEN LOOKING BACK ON HOW I'VE RATED MY WEEKS THUS FAR, THE NUMBERS TELL ME

MY INTENTION FOR THE NEXT THREE MONTHS

WHO HAVE I BEEN UNABLE TO FEEL GRATEFUL FOR DURING THE PAST THREE MONTHS? CAN I REFORMULATE THAT THOUGHT ANYWAY? I AM GRATEFUL...

DAY 92

THREE THINGS I'M GRATEFUL FOR

I GIVE TODAY A

SOMETHING I WANT TO REMEMBER ABOUT TODAY

SOMETHING I COULD HAVE BEEN MORE GRATEFUL FOR TODAY

MY INTENTION FOR TOMORROW

DAY 93

THREE THINGS I'M GRATEFUL FOR

SOMETHING I WANT TO REMEMBER ABOUT TODAY

I GIVE TODAY A

MY INTENTION FOR
TOMORROW

SOMETHING I COULD HAVE BEEN MORE GRATEFUL FOR TODAY

DAY 94

DAY   MONTH   YEAR

THREE THINGS I'M GRATEFUL FOR

I GIVE TODAY A

SOMETHING I WANT TO REMEMBER ABOUT TODAY

SOMETHING I COULD HAVE BEEN MORE GRATEFUL FOR TODAY

MY INTENTION FOR TOMORROW

Day 95

Day   Month   Year

Three things I'm grateful for

Something I want to remember about today   I give today a

My intention for   Something I could have been more grateful for today
tomorrow

DAY 96

DAY   MONTH   YEAR

THREE THINGS I'M GRATEFUL FOR

I GIVE TODAY A   SOMETHING I WANT TO REMEMBER ABOUT TODAY

SOMETHING I COULD HAVE BEEN MORE GRATEFUL FOR TODAY   MY INTENTION FOR
TOMORROW

Day 97

Month   Year

Three things I'm grateful for

Something I want to remember about today

I give today a

My intention for
tomorrow

Something I could have been more grateful for today

DAY 98

DAY   MONTH   YEAR

THREE THINGS I'M GRATEFUL FOR

I GIVE TODAY A

SOMETHING I WANT TO REMEMBER ABOUT TODAY

SOMETHING I COULD HAVE BEEN MORE GRATEFUL FOR TODAY

MY INTENTION FOR TOMORROW

DAY 98

'THANK YOU' IS THE BEST PRAYER THAT ANYONE COULD SAY. I SAY THAT ONE A LOT. THANK YOU EXPRESSES EXTREME GRATITUDE, HUMILITY, UNDERSTANDING.

ALICE WALKER

SOMETHING I COULD HAVE BEEN MORE GRATEFUL FOR THIS WEEK

I GIVE THIS WEEK A

SOMETHING I WANT TO REMEMBER ABOUT THIS WEEK

MY INTENTION FOR NEXT WEEK

SOMEONE I COULD HAVE FELT MORE GRATEFUL FOR THIS WEEK

DAY 99

DAY   MONTH   YEAR

THREE THINGS I'M GRATEFUL FOR

I GIVE TODAY A

SOMETHING I WANT TO REMEMBER ABOUT TODAY

SOMETHING I COULD HAVE BEEN MORE GRATEFUL FOR TODAY

MY INTENTION FOR TOMORROW

DAY 100

Day   Month   Year

THREE THINGS I'M GRATEFUL FOR

SOMETHING I WANT TO REMEMBER ABOUT TODAY

I GIVE TODAY A

MY INTENTION FOR
TOMORROW

SOMETHING I COULD HAVE BEEN MORE GRATEFUL FOR TODAY

DAY 101

DAY   MONTH   YEAR

THREE THINGS I'M GRATEFUL FOR

I GIVE TODAY A

SOMETHING I WANT TO REMEMBER ABOUT TODAY

SOMETHING I COULD HAVE BEEN MORE GRATEFUL FOR TODAY

MY INTENTION FOR TOMORROW

DAY 102

Month

Year

Three things I'm grateful for

Something I want to remember about today

I give today a

My intention for
tomorrow

Something I could have been more grateful for today

DAY 103

DAY   MONTH   YEAR

THREE THINGS I'M GRATEFUL FOR

I GIVE TODAY A   SOMETHING I WANT TO REMEMBER ABOUT TODAY

SOMETHING I COULD HAVE BEEN MORE GRATEFUL FOR TODAY   MY INTENTION FOR
                    TOMORROW

DAY 104

THREE THINGS I'M GRATEFUL FOR

SOMETHING I WANT TO REMEMBER ABOUT TODAY

I GIVE TODAY A

MY INTENTION FOR TOMORROW

SOMETHING I COULD HAVE BEEN MORE GRATEFUL FOR TODAY

DAY 105

DAY   MONTH   YEAR

THREE THINGS I'M GRATEFUL FOR

I GIVE TODAY A

SOMETHING I WANT TO REMEMBER ABOUT TODAY

SOMETHING I COULD HAVE BEEN MORE GRATEFUL FOR TODAY

MY INTENTION FOR TOMORROW

DAY 105

GRATITUDE IS THE ABILITY TO EXPERIENCE LIFE AS A GIFT. IT LIBERATES US FROM THE PRISON OF SELF-PREOCCUPATION.

JOHN ORTBERG

SOMETHING I COULD HAVE BEEN MORE GRATEFUL FOR THIS WEEK

I GIVE THIS WEEK A

SOMETHING I WANT TO REMEMBER ABOUT THIS WEEK

MY INTENTION FOR NEXT WEEK

SOMEONE I COULD HAVE FELT MORE GRATEFUL FOR THIS WEEK

DAY 106

DAY MONTH YEAR

THREE THINGS I'M GRATEFUL FOR

I GIVE TODAY A   SOMETHING I WANT TO REMEMBER ABOUT TODAY

SOMETHING I COULD HAVE BEEN MORE GRATEFUL FOR TODAY MY INTENTION FOR TOMORROW

DAY 107

Three things I'm grateful for

Something I want to remember about today

I give today a

My intention for tomorrow

Something I could have been more grateful for today

DAY 108

THREE THINGS I'M GRATEFUL FOR

I GIVE TODAY A

SOMETHING I WANT TO REMEMBER ABOUT TODAY

SOMETHING I COULD HAVE BEEN MORE GRATEFUL FOR TODAY

MY INTENTION FOR TOMORROW

DAY 109

Day   Month   Year

Three things I'm grateful for

Something I want to remember about today

I give today a

My intention for
tomorrow

Something I could have been more grateful for today

DAY 110

DAY   MONTH   YEAR

THREE THINGS I'M GRATEFUL FOR

I GIVE TODAY A

SOMETHING I WANT TO REMEMBER ABOUT TODAY

SOMETHING I COULD HAVE BEEN MORE GRATEFUL FOR TODAY

MY INTENTION FOR TOMORROW

DAY 111

Day   Month   Year

Three things I'm grateful for

Something I want to remember about today

I give today a

My intention for
tomorrow

Something I could have been more grateful for today

DAY 112

DAY   MONTH   YEAR

THREE THINGS I'M GRATEFUL FOR

I GIVE TODAY A

SOMETHING I WANT TO REMEMBER ABOUT TODAY

SOMETHING I COULD HAVE BEEN MORE GRATEFUL FOR TODAY

MY INTENTION FOR TOMORROW

DAY 112

When some things go wrong, take a moment to be thankful for the many things that are going right.

Annie Gottlier

Something I could have been more grateful for these past four weeks

I give the past four weeks a

Something I want to remember about the past four weeks

My intention for the next four weeks

Someone I could have felt more grateful for these past four weeks

DAY 113

THREE THINGS I'M GRATEFUL FOR

I GIVE TODAY A

SOMETHING I WANT TO REMEMBER ABOUT TODAY

SOMETHING I COULD HAVE BEEN MORE GRATEFUL FOR TODAY

MY INTENTION FOR TOMORROW

Day 114

Day   Month   Year

Three things I'm grateful for

Something I want to remember about today

I give today a

My intention for
tomorrow

Something I could have been more grateful for today

DAY 115

DAY   MONTH   YEAR

THREE THINGS I'M GRATEFUL FOR

I GIVE TODAY A   SOMETHING I WANT TO REMEMBER ABOUT TODAY

SOMETHING I COULD HAVE BEEN MORE GRATEFUL FOR TODAY   MY INTENTION FOR
TOMORROW

DAY 116

DAY   MONTH   YEAR

THREE THINGS I'M GRATEFUL FOR

SOMETHING I WANT TO REMEMBER ABOUT TODAY

I GIVE TODAY A

MY INTENTION FOR
TOMORROW

SOMETHING I COULD HAVE BEEN MORE GRATEFUL FOR TODAY

DAY 117

DAY   MONTH   YEAR

THREE THINGS I'M GRATEFUL FOR

I GIVE TODAY A   SOMETHING I WANT TO REMEMBER ABOUT TODAY

SOMETHING I COULD HAVE BEEN MORE GRATEFUL FOR TODAY   MY INTENTION FOR
TOMORROW

Day 118

Three things I'm grateful for

Something I want to remember about today

I give today a

My intention for tomorrow

Something I could have been more grateful for today

DAY 119

DAY   MONTH   YEAR

THREE THINGS I'M GRATEFUL FOR

I GIVE TODAY A

SOMETHING I WANT TO REMEMBER ABOUT TODAY

SOMETHING I COULD HAVE BEEN MORE GRATEFUL FOR TODAY

MY INTENTION FOR TOMORROW

DAY 119

IF YOU CONCENTRATE ON FINDING WHATEVER IS GOOD IN EVERY SITUATION,
YOU WILL DISCOVER THAT YOUR LIFE WILL SUDDENLY BE FILLED WITH GRATITUDE,
A FEELING THAT NURTURES THE SOUL.

RABBI HAROLD KUSHNER

SOMETHING I COULD HAVE BEEN MORE GRATEFUL FOR THIS WEEK

I GIVE THIS WEEK A

SOMETHING I WANT TO REMEMBER ABOUT THIS WEEK

MY INTENTION FOR NEXT WEEK

SOMEONE I COULD HAVE FELT MORE GRATEFUL FOR THIS WEEK

DAY 120

DAY   MONTH   YEAR

THREE THINGS I'M GRATEFUL FOR

I GIVE TODAY A

SOMETHING I WANT TO REMEMBER ABOUT TODAY

SOMETHING I COULD HAVE BEEN MORE GRATEFUL FOR TODAY

MY INTENTION FOR
TOMORROW

DAY 121

Day   Month   Year

Three things I'm grateful for

Something I want to remember about today

I give today a

My intention for tomorrow

Something I could have been more grateful for today

DAY 122

DAY   MONTH   YEAR

THREE THINGS I'M GRATEFUL FOR

I GIVE TODAY A

SOMETHING I WANT TO REMEMBER ABOUT TODAY

SOMETHING I COULD HAVE BEEN MORE GRATEFUL FOR TODAY

MY INTENTION FOR TOMORROW

DAY 123

DAY   MONTH   YEAR

THREE THINGS I'M GRATEFUL FOR

SOMETHING I WANT TO REMEMBER ABOUT TODAY   I GIVE TODAY A

MY INTENTION FOR TOMORROW   SOMETHING I COULD HAVE BEEN MORE GRATEFUL FOR TODAY

DAY 124

DAY   MONTH   YEAR

THREE THINGS I'M GRATEFUL FOR

I GIVE TODAY A

SOMETHING I WANT TO REMEMBER ABOUT TODAY

SOMETHING I COULD HAVE BEEN MORE GRATEFUL FOR TODAY

MY INTENTION FOR TOMORROW

Day 125

Day   Month   Year

Three things I'm grateful for

Something I want to remember about today

I give today a

My intention for tomorrow

Something I could have been more grateful for today

DAY 126

THREE THINGS I'M GRATEFUL FOR

I GIVE TODAY A

SOMETHING I WANT TO REMEMBER ABOUT TODAY

SOMETHING I COULD HAVE BEEN MORE GRATEFUL FOR TODAY

MY INTENTION FOR TOMORROW

DAY 126

Be thankful for what you have; you'll end up having more.
If you concentrate on what you don't have, you will never,
ever have enough.

Oprah Winfrey

Something I could have been more grateful for this week

I give this week a

Something I want to remember about this week

My intention for next week

Someone I could have felt more grateful for this week

DAY 127

DAY   MONTH   YEAR

THREE THINGS I'M GRATEFUL FOR

I GIVE TODAY A

SOMETHING I WANT TO REMEMBER ABOUT TODAY

SOMETHING I COULD HAVE BEEN MORE GRATEFUL FOR TODAY

MY INTENTION FOR TOMORROW

DAY 128

DAY   MONTH   YEAR

THREE THINGS I'M GRATEFUL FOR

SOMETHING I WANT TO REMEMBER ABOUT TODAY

I GIVE TODAY A

MY INTENTION FOR TOMORROW

SOMETHING I COULD HAVE BEEN MORE GRATEFUL FOR TODAY

DAY 129

Day   Month   Year

Three things I'm grateful for

I give today a

Something I want to remember about today

Something I could have been more grateful for today

My intention for tomorrow

DAY 130

Day   Month   Year

Three things I'm grateful for

Something I want to remember about today   I give today a

My intention for
tomorrow   Something I could have been more grateful for today

DAY 131

DAY   MONTH   YEAR

THREE THINGS I'M GRATEFUL FOR

I GIVE TODAY A

SOMETHING I WANT TO REMEMBER ABOUT TODAY

SOMETHING I COULD HAVE BEEN MORE GRATEFUL FOR TODAY

MY INTENTION FOR
TOMORROW

DAY 132

THREE THINGS I'M GRATEFUL FOR

SOMETHING I WANT TO REMEMBER ABOUT TODAY

I GIVE TODAY A

MY INTENTION FOR TOMORROW

SOMETHING I COULD HAVE BEEN MORE GRATEFUL FOR TODAY

DAY 133

Day   Month   Year

Three things I'm grateful for

I give today a

Something I want to remember about today

Something I could have been more grateful for today

My intention for tomorrow

DAY 133

Thankfulness is the beginning of gratitude. Gratitude is the completion of thankfulness. Thankfulness may consist merely of words. Gratitude is shown in acts.

Henri-Frédéric Amiel

Something I could have been more grateful for this week

I give this week a

Something I want to remember about this week

My intention for next week

Someone I could have felt more grateful for this week

DAY 134

DAY   MONTH   YEAR

THREE THINGS I'M GRATEFUL FOR

I GIVE TODAY A

SOMETHING I WANT TO REMEMBER ABOUT TODAY

SOMETHING I COULD HAVE BEEN MORE GRATEFUL FOR TODAY

MY INTENTION FOR TOMORROW

Day 135

Day   Month   Year

Three things I'm grateful for

Something I want to remember about today

I give today a

My intention for tomorrow

Something I could have been more grateful for today

DAY 136

DAY   MONTH   YEAR

THREE THINGS I'M GRATEFUL FOR

I GIVE TODAY A   SOMETHING I WANT TO REMEMBER ABOUT TODAY

SOMETHING I COULD HAVE BEEN MORE GRATEFUL FOR TODAY   MY INTENTION FOR TOMORROW

DAY 137

DAY   MONTH   YEAR

THREE THINGS I'M GRATEFUL FOR

SOMETHING I WANT TO REMEMBER ABOUT TODAY   I GIVE TODAY A

MY INTENTION FOR
TOMORROW   SOMETHING I COULD HAVE BEEN MORE GRATEFUL FOR TODAY

DAY 138

THREE THINGS I'M GRATEFUL FOR

I GIVE TODAY A   SOMETHING I WANT TO REMEMBER ABOUT TODAY

SOMETHING I COULD HAVE BEEN MORE GRATEFUL FOR TODAY   MY INTENTION FOR
TOMORROW

Day 139

Day   Month   Year

Three things I'm grateful for

Something I want to remember about today

I give today a

My intention for tomorrow

Something I could have been more grateful for today

DAY 140

MONTH

YEAR

THREE THINGS I'M GRATEFUL FOR

I GIVE TODAY A

SOMETHING I WANT TO REMEMBER ABOUT TODAY

SOMETHING I COULD HAVE BEEN MORE GRATEFUL FOR TODAY

MY INTENTION FOR
TOMORROW

DAY 140

THE MORE GRATEFUL I AM, THE MORE BEAUTY I SEE.

MARY DAVIS

SOMETHING I COULD HAVE BEEN MORE GRATEFUL FOR THESE PAST FOUR WEEKS

I GIVE THE PAST FOUR WEEKS A

SOMETHING I WANT TO REMEMBER ABOUT THE PAST FOUR WEEKS

MY INTENTION FOR THE NEXT FOUR WEEKS

SOMEONE I COULD HAVE FELT MORE GRATEFUL FOR THESE PAST FOUR WEEKS

DAY 141

DAY   MONTH   YEAR

THREE THINGS I'M GRATEFUL FOR

I GIVE TODAY A

SOMETHING I WANT TO REMEMBER ABOUT TODAY

SOMETHING I COULD HAVE BEEN MORE GRATEFUL FOR TODAY

MY INTENTION FOR TOMORROW

DAY 142

Three things I'm grateful for

Something I want to remember about today

I give today a

My intention for tomorrow

Something I could have been more grateful for today

DAY 143

Day   Month   Year

Three things I'm grateful for

I give today a

Something I want to remember about today

Something I could have been more grateful for today

My intention for tomorrow

DAY 144

THREE THINGS I'M GRATEFUL FOR

SOMETHING I WANT TO REMEMBER ABOUT TODAY

I GIVE TODAY A

MY INTENTION FOR
TOMORROW

SOMETHING I COULD HAVE BEEN MORE GRATEFUL FOR TODAY

DAY 145

DAY   MONTH   YEAR

THREE THINGS I'M GRATEFUL FOR

I GIVE TODAY A

SOMETHING I WANT TO REMEMBER ABOUT TODAY

SOMETHING I COULD HAVE BEEN MORE GRATEFUL FOR TODAY

MY INTENTION FOR
TOMORROW

Day 146

Three things I'm grateful for

Something I want to remember about today

I give today a

My intention for
tomorrow

Something I could have been more grateful for today

DAY 147

DAY   MONTH   YEAR

THREE THINGS I'M GRATEFUL FOR

I GIVE TODAY A

SOMETHING I WANT TO REMEMBER ABOUT TODAY

SOMETHING I COULD HAVE BEEN MORE GRATEFUL FOR TODAY

MY INTENTION FOR
TOMORROW

Day 147

Gratitude + Generosity = Abundance

Unknown

Something I could have been more grateful for this week

I give this week a

Something I want to remember about this week

My intention for next week

Someone I could have felt more grateful for this week

DAY 148

DAY   MONTH   YEAR

THREE THINGS I'M GRATEFUL FOR

I GIVE TODAY A

SOMETHING I WANT TO REMEMBER ABOUT TODAY

SOMETHING I COULD HAVE BEEN MORE GRATEFUL FOR TODAY

MY INTENTION FOR TOMORROW

Day 149

Day   Month   Year

Three things I'm grateful for

Something I want to remember about today

I give today a

My intention for tomorrow

Something I could have been more grateful for today

DAY 150

DAY   MONTH   YEAR

THREE THINGS I'M GRATEFUL FOR

I GIVE TODAY A

SOMETHING I WANT TO REMEMBER ABOUT TODAY

SOMETHING I COULD HAVE BEEN MORE GRATEFUL FOR TODAY

MY INTENTION FOR TOMORROW

DAY 151

Day   Month   Year

Three things I'm grateful for

Something I want to remember about today   I give today a

My intention for   Something I could have been more grateful for today
tomorrow

DAY 152

THREE THINGS I'M GRATEFUL FOR

I GIVE TODAY A

SOMETHING I WANT TO REMEMBER ABOUT TODAY

SOMETHING I COULD HAVE BEEN MORE GRATEFUL FOR TODAY

MY INTENTION FOR
TOMORROW

DAY 153

MONTH

YEAR

THREE THINGS I'M GRATEFUL FOR

SOMETHING I WANT TO REMEMBER ABOUT TODAY

I GIVE TODAY A

MY INTENTION FOR
TOMORROW

SOMETHING I COULD HAVE BEEN MORE GRATEFUL FOR TODAY

DAY 154

Day   Month   Year

Three things I'm grateful for

I give today a

Something I want to remember about today

Something I could have been more grateful for today

My intention for tomorrow

DAY 154

WHEN GRATITUDE BECOMES AN ESSENTIAL FOUNDATION IN OUR LIVES, MIRACLES START TO APPEAR EVERYWHERE.

Emmanuel Dagher

SOMETHING I COULD HAVE BEEN MORE GRATEFUL FOR THIS WEEK

I GIVE THIS WEEK A

SOMETHING I WANT TO REMEMBER ABOUT THIS WEEK

MY INTENTION FOR NEXT WEEK

SOMEONE I COULD HAVE FELT MORE GRATEFUL FOR THIS WEEK

DAY 155

THREE THINGS I'M GRATEFUL FOR

I GIVE TODAY A

SOMETHING I WANT TO REMEMBER ABOUT TODAY

SOMETHING I COULD HAVE BEEN MORE GRATEFUL FOR TODAY

MY INTENTION FOR TOMORROW

DAY 156

THREE THINGS I'M GRATEFUL FOR

SOMETHING I WANT TO REMEMBER ABOUT TODAY   I GIVE TODAY A

MY INTENTION FOR
TOMORROW   SOMETHING I COULD HAVE BEEN MORE GRATEFUL FOR TODAY

DAY 157

DAY   MONTH   YEAR

THREE THINGS I'M GRATEFUL FOR

I GIVE TODAY A   SOMETHING I WANT TO REMEMBER ABOUT TODAY

SOMETHING I COULD HAVE BEEN MORE GRATEFUL FOR TODAY   MY INTENTION FOR
TOMORROW

DAY 158

THREE THINGS I'M GRATEFUL FOR

SOMETHING I WANT TO REMEMBER ABOUT TODAY

I GIVE TODAY A

MY INTENTION FOR
TOMORROW

SOMETHING I COULD HAVE BEEN MORE GRATEFUL FOR TODAY

DAY 159

DAY   MONTH   YEAR

THREE THINGS I'M GRATEFUL FOR

I GIVE TODAY A

SOMETHING I WANT TO REMEMBER ABOUT TODAY

SOMETHING I COULD HAVE BEEN MORE GRATEFUL FOR TODAY

MY INTENTION FOR TOMORROW

DAY 160

Three things I'm grateful for

Something I want to remember about today

I give today a

My intention for tomorrow

Something I could have been more grateful for today

DAY 161

DAY   MONTH   YEAR

THREE THINGS I'M GRATEFUL FOR

I GIVE TODAY A   SOMETHING I WANT TO REMEMBER ABOUT TODAY

SOMETHING I COULD HAVE BEEN MORE GRATEFUL FOR TODAY   MY INTENTION FOR TOMORROW

DAY 161

COUNT YOUR RAINBOWS, NOT YOUR THUNDERSTORMS.

Alyssa Knight

SOMETHING I COULD HAVE BEEN MORE GRATEFUL FOR THIS WEEK

I GIVE THIS WEEK A

SOMETHING I WANT TO REMEMBER ABOUT THIS WEEK

MY INTENTION FOR NEXT WEEK

SOMEONE I COULD HAVE FELT MORE GRATEFUL FOR THIS WEEK

DAY 162

DAY   MONTH   YEAR

THREE THINGS I'M GRATEFUL FOR

I GIVE TODAY A

SOMETHING I WANT TO REMEMBER ABOUT TODAY

SOMETHING I COULD HAVE BEEN MORE GRATEFUL FOR TODAY

MY INTENTION FOR TOMORROW

DAY 163

THREE THINGS I'M GRATEFUL FOR

SOMETHING I WANT TO REMEMBER ABOUT TODAY

I GIVE TODAY A

MY INTENTION FOR
TOMORROW

SOMETHING I COULD HAVE BEEN MORE GRATEFUL FOR TODAY

DAY 164

DAY   MONTH   YEAR

THREE THINGS I'M GRATEFUL FOR

I GIVE TODAY A

SOMETHING I WANT TO REMEMBER ABOUT TODAY

SOMETHING I COULD HAVE BEEN MORE GRATEFUL FOR TODAY

MY INTENTION FOR
TOMORROW

DAY 165

Day   Month   Year

Three things I'm grateful for

Something I want to remember about today   I give today a

My intention for   Something I could have been more grateful for today
tomorrow

DAY 166

DAY   MONTH   YEAR

THREE THINGS I'M GRATEFUL FOR

I GIVE TODAY A

SOMETHING I WANT TO REMEMBER ABOUT TODAY

SOMETHING I COULD HAVE BEEN MORE GRATEFUL FOR TODAY

MY INTENTION FOR TOMORROW

Day 167

Three things I'm grateful for

Something I want to remember about today

I give today a

My intention for tomorrow

Something I could have been more grateful for today

DAY 168

THREE THINGS I'M GRATEFUL FOR

I GIVE TODAY A   SOMETHING I WANT TO REMEMBER ABOUT TODAY

SOMETHING I COULD HAVE BEEN MORE GRATEFUL FOR TODAY   MY INTENTION FOR
TOMORROW

DAY 168

If the only prayer we every say in our lives is 'Thank you', it will be enough.

Meister Eckhart

SOMETHING I COULD HAVE BEEN MORE GRATEFUL FOR THESE PAST FOUR WEEKS

I GIVE THE PAST FOUR WEEKS A

SOMETHING I WANT TO REMEMBER ABOUT THE PAST FOUR WEEKS

MY INTENTION FOR THE NEXT FOUR WEEKS

SOMEONE I COULD HAVE FELT MORE GRATEFUL FOR THESE PAST FOUR WEEKS

DAY 169

DAY   MONTH   YEAR

THREE THINGS I'M GRATEFUL FOR

I GIVE TODAY A   SOMETHING I WANT TO REMEMBER ABOUT TODAY

SOMETHING I COULD HAVE BEEN MORE GRATEFUL FOR TODAY   MY INTENTION FOR TOMORROW

Day 170

Three things I'm grateful for

Something I want to remember about today

I give today a

My intention for
tomorrow

Something I could have been more grateful for today

DAY 171

THREE THINGS I'M GRATEFUL FOR

I GIVE TODAY A

SOMETHING I WANT TO REMEMBER ABOUT TODAY

SOMETHING I COULD HAVE BEEN MORE GRATEFUL FOR TODAY

MY INTENTION FOR TOMORROW

DAY 172

Day   Month   Year

Three things I'm grateful for

Something I want to remember about today   I give today a

My intention for
tomorrow   Something I could have been more grateful for today

DAY 173

DAY   MONTH   YEAR

THREE THINGS I'M GRATEFUL FOR

I GIVE TODAY A

SOMETHING I WANT TO REMEMBER ABOUT TODAY

SOMETHING I COULD HAVE BEEN MORE GRATEFUL FOR TODAY

MY INTENTION FOR TOMORROW

DAY 174

DAY   MONTH   YEAR

THREE THINGS I'M GRATEFUL FOR

SOMETHING I WANT TO REMEMBER ABOUT TODAY

I GIVE TODAY A

MY INTENTION FOR TOMORROW

SOMETHING I COULD HAVE BEEN MORE GRATEFUL FOR TODAY

DAY 175

DAY   MONTH   YEAR

THREE THINGS I'M GRATEFUL FOR

I GIVE TODAY A   SOMETHING I WANT TO REMEMBER ABOUT TODAY

SOMETHING I COULD HAVE BEEN MORE GRATEFUL FOR TODAY   MY INTENTION FOR TOMORROW

DAY 175

WE'RE A NATION HUNGRY FOR MORE JOY,
BECAUSE WE'RE STARVING FROM A LACK OF GRATITUDE.

BRENÉ BROWN

SOMETHING I COULD HAVE BEEN MORE GRATEFUL FOR THIS WEEK

I GIVE THIS WEEK A

SOMETHING I WANT TO REMEMBER ABOUT THIS WEEK

MY INTENTION FOR NEXT WEEK

SOMEONE I COULD HAVE FELT MORE GRATEFUL FOR THIS WEEK

DAY 176

THREE THINGS I'M GRATEFUL FOR

I GIVE TODAY A

SOMETHING I WANT TO REMEMBER ABOUT TODAY

SOMETHING I COULD HAVE BEEN MORE GRATEFUL FOR TODAY

MY INTENTION FOR TOMORROW

Day 177

Day   Month   Year

Three things I'm grateful for

Something I want to remember about today

I give today a

My intention for tomorrow

Something I could have been more grateful for today

DAY 178

DAY   MONTH   YEAR

THREE THINGS I'M GRATEFUL FOR

I GIVE TODAY A

SOMETHING I WANT TO REMEMBER ABOUT TODAY

SOMETHING I COULD HAVE BEEN MORE GRATEFUL FOR TODAY

MY INTENTION FOR TOMORROW

DAY 179

DAY   MONTH   YEAR

Three things I'm grateful for

Something I want to remember about today

I give today a

My intention for
tomorrow

Something I could have been more grateful for today

DAY 180

THREE THINGS I'M GRATEFUL FOR

I GIVE TODAY A

SOMETHING I WANT TO REMEMBER ABOUT TODAY

SOMETHING I COULD HAVE BEEN MORE GRATEFUL FOR TODAY

MY INTENTION FOR
TOMORROW

DAY 181

Three things I'm grateful for

Something I want to remember about today

I give today a

My intention for tomorrow

Something I could have been more grateful for today

DAY 182

THREE THINGS I'M GRATEFUL FOR

I GIVE TODAY A   SOMETHING I WANT TO REMEMBER ABOUT TODAY

SOMETHING I COULD HAVE BEEN MORE GRATEFUL FOR TODAY   MY INTENTION FOR
TOMORROW

DAY 182

We should certainly count our blessings, but we should also make our blessings count.

Neal A. Maxwell

Something I could have been more grateful for this week

I give this week a

Something I want to remember about this week

My intention for next week

Someone I could have felt more grateful for this week

Let's look back again. Go over the past thirteen weeks, then answer the following:

Something I want to remember about the past three months

Looking back over the past three months, I am most grateful for

The biggest lesson I learned over the past three months

Someone or something I could have felt more grateful for during the past three months

6 MONTHS

I GIVE THE PAST THREE MONTHS A

WHAT HAVE I BEEN UNABLE TO FEEL GRATEFUL FOR DURING THE PAST THREE MONTHS? CAN I REFORMULATE THAT THOUGHT ANYWAY?

I AM GRATEFUL....

WHEN LOOKING BACK ON HOW I'VE RATED MY WEEKS THUS FAR, THE NUMBERS TELL ME

MY INTENTION FOR THE NEXT THREE MONTHS

WHO HAVE I BEEN UNABLE TO FEEL GRATEFUL FOR DURING THE PAST THREE MONTHS? CAN I REFORMULATE THAT THOUGHT ANYWAY? I AM GRATEFUL....

DAY 183

DAY   MONTH   YEAR

Three things I'm grateful for

I give today a

Something I want to remember about today

Something I could have been more grateful for today

My intention for tomorrow

DAY 184

Day   Month   Year

Three things I'm grateful for

Something I want to remember about today

I give today a

My intention for tomorrow

Something I could have been more grateful for today

DAY 185

DAY   MONTH   YEAR

THREE THINGS I'M GRATEFUL FOR

I GIVE TODAY A

SOMETHING I WANT TO REMEMBER ABOUT TODAY

SOMETHING I COULD HAVE BEEN MORE GRATEFUL FOR TODAY

MY INTENTION FOR TOMORROW

DAY 186

THREE THINGS I'M GRATEFUL FOR

SOMETHING I WANT TO REMEMBER ABOUT TODAY

I GIVE TODAY A

MY INTENTION FOR
TOMORROW

SOMETHING I COULD HAVE BEEN MORE GRATEFUL FOR TODAY

DAY 187

DAY   MONTH   YEAR

THREE THINGS I'M GRATEFUL FOR

I GIVE TODAY A

SOMETHING I WANT TO REMEMBER ABOUT TODAY

SOMETHING I COULD HAVE BEEN MORE GRATEFUL FOR TODAY

MY INTENTION FOR TOMORROW

DAY 188

Three things I'm grateful for

Something I want to remember about today

I give today a

My intention for tomorrow

Something I could have been more grateful for today

DAY 189

DAY   MONTH   YEAR

Three things I'm grateful for

I GIVE TODAY A   SOMETHING I WANT TO REMEMBER ABOUT TODAY

SOMETHING I COULD HAVE BEEN MORE GRATEFUL FOR TODAY   MY INTENTION FOR TOMORROW

DAY 189

THE MORE THAT WE FEEL GRATEFUL IN OUR LIVES, THE MORE JOY AND FULFILLMENT WE'RE ABLE TO FEEL.

MIRANDA ANDERSON

SOMETHING I COULD HAVE BEEN MORE GRATEFUL FOR THIS WEEK

I GIVE THIS WEEK A

SOMETHING I WANT TO REMEMBER ABOUT THIS WEEK

MY INTENTION FOR NEXT WEEK

SOMEONE I COULD HAVE FELT MORE GRATEFUL FOR THIS WEEK

DAY 190

DAY   MONTH   YEAR

THREE THINGS I'M GRATEFUL FOR

I GIVE TODAY A   SOMETHING I WANT TO REMEMBER ABOUT TODAY

SOMETHING I COULD HAVE BEEN MORE GRATEFUL FOR TODAY   MY INTENTION FOR TOMORROW

Day 191

Three things I'm grateful for

Something I want to remember about today

I give today a

My intention for
tomorrow

Something I could have been more grateful for today

DAY 192

DAY   MONTH   YEAR

THREE THINGS I'M GRATEFUL FOR

I GIVE TODAY A

SOMETHING I WANT TO REMEMBER ABOUT TODAY

SOMETHING I COULD HAVE BEEN MORE GRATEFUL FOR TODAY

MY INTENTION FOR TOMORROW

Day 193

Three things I'm grateful for

Something I want to remember about today

I give today a

My intention for tomorrow

Something I could have been more grateful for today

DAY 194

DAY   MONTH   YEAR

THREE THINGS I'M GRATEFUL FOR

I GIVE TODAY A

SOMETHING I WANT TO REMEMBER ABOUT TODAY

SOMETHING I COULD HAVE BEEN MORE GRATEFUL FOR TODAY

MY INTENTION FOR TOMORROW

DAY 195

THREE THINGS I'M GRATEFUL FOR

SOMETHING I WANT TO REMEMBER ABOUT TODAY

I GIVE TODAY A

MY INTENTION FOR
TOMORROW

SOMETHING I COULD HAVE BEEN MORE GRATEFUL FOR TODAY

DAY 196

THREE THINGS I'M GRATEFUL FOR

I GIVE TODAY A   SOMETHING I WANT TO REMEMBER ABOUT TODAY

SOMETHING I COULD HAVE BEEN MORE GRATEFUL FOR TODAY   MY INTENTION FOR
TOMORROW

DAY 196

Do not spoil what you have by desiring what you have not;
remember that what you now have was once among the things
you only hoped for.

Epicurus

Something I could have been more grateful for these
past four weeks

I give the past four weeks a

Something I want to remember about the past four weeks

My intention for the
next four weeks

Someone I could have felt more grateful for these past
four weeks

DAY 197

DAY   MONTH   YEAR

THREE THINGS I'M GRATEFUL FOR

I GIVE TODAY A

SOMETHING I WANT TO REMEMBER ABOUT TODAY

SOMETHING I COULD HAVE BEEN MORE GRATEFUL FOR TODAY

MY INTENTION FOR TOMORROW

DAY 198

THREE THINGS I'M GRATEFUL FOR

SOMETHING I WANT TO REMEMBER ABOUT TODAY

I GIVE TODAY A

MY INTENTION FOR
TOMORROW

SOMETHING I COULD HAVE BEEN MORE GRATEFUL FOR TODAY

DAY 199

DAY   MONTH   YEAR

THREE THINGS I'M GRATEFUL FOR

I GIVE TODAY A

SOMETHING I WANT TO REMEMBER ABOUT TODAY

SOMETHING I COULD HAVE BEEN MORE GRATEFUL FOR TODAY

MY INTENTION FOR TOMORROW

DAY 200

THREE THINGS I'M GRATEFUL FOR

SOMETHING I WANT TO REMEMBER ABOUT TODAY

I GIVE TODAY A

MY INTENTION FOR
TOMORROW

SOMETHING I COULD HAVE BEEN MORE GRATEFUL FOR TODAY

DAY 201

THREE THINGS I'M GRATEFUL FOR

I GIVE TODAY A

SOMETHING I WANT TO REMEMBER ABOUT TODAY

SOMETHING I COULD HAVE BEEN MORE GRATEFUL FOR TODAY

MY INTENTION FOR
TOMORROW

DAY 202

Three things I'm grateful for

Something I want to remember about today

I give today a

My intention for
tomorrow

Something I could have been more grateful for today

DAY 203

THREE THINGS I'M GRATEFUL FOR

I GIVE TODAY A   SOMETHING I WANT TO REMEMBER ABOUT TODAY

SOMETHING I COULD HAVE BEEN MORE GRATEFUL FOR TODAY   MY INTENTION FOR
TOMORROW

DAY 203

THE ACT OF BEING GRATEFUL IS THE DOOR THAT LEADS TO ALL THINGS BEAUTIFUL IN LIFE.

UNKNOWN

SOMETHING I COULD HAVE BEEN MORE GRATEFUL FOR THIS WEEK

I GIVE THIS WEEK A

SOMETHING I WANT TO REMEMBER ABOUT THIS WEEK

MY INTENTION FOR NEXT WEEK

SOMEONE I COULD HAVE FELT MORE GRATEFUL FOR THIS WEEK

DAY 204

DAY   MONTH   YEAR

THREE THINGS I'M GRATEFUL FOR

I GIVE TODAY A

SOMETHING I WANT TO REMEMBER ABOUT TODAY

SOMETHING I COULD HAVE BEEN MORE GRATEFUL FOR TODAY

MY INTENTION FOR TOMORROW

DAY 205

Three things I'm grateful for

Something I want to remember about today

I give today a

My intention for tomorrow

Something I could have been more grateful for today

DAY 206

DAY   MONTH   YEAR

THREE THINGS I'M GRATEFUL FOR

I GIVE TODAY A

SOMETHING I WANT TO REMEMBER ABOUT TODAY

SOMETHING I COULD HAVE BEEN MORE GRATEFUL FOR TODAY

MY INTENTION FOR TOMORROW

Day 207

Day   Month   Year

Three things I'm grateful for

Something I want to remember about today

I give today a

My intention for
tomorrow

Something I could have been more grateful for today

DAY 208

THREE THINGS I'M GRATEFUL FOR

I GIVE TODAY A   SOMETHING I WANT TO REMEMBER ABOUT TODAY

SOMETHING I COULD HAVE BEEN MORE GRATEFUL FOR TODAY   MY INTENTION FOR
TOMORROW

DAY 209

THREE THINGS I'M GRATEFUL FOR

SOMETHING I WANT TO REMEMBER ABOUT TODAY

I GIVE TODAY A

MY INTENTION FOR
TOMORROW

SOMETHING I COULD HAVE BEEN MORE GRATEFUL FOR TODAY

DAY 210

DAY   MONTH   YEAR

THREE THINGS I'M GRATEFUL FOR

I GIVE TODAY A   SOMETHING I WANT TO REMEMBER ABOUT TODAY

SOMETHING I COULD HAVE BEEN MORE GRATEFUL FOR TODAY   MY INTENTION FOR
TOMORROW

DAY 210

GRATITUDE IS AN ESSENTIAL PART OF BEING PRESENT. WHEN YOU GO DEEPLY INTO THE PRESENT, GRATITUDE ARISES SPONTANEOUSLY.

Eckhart Tolle

SOMETHING I COULD HAVE BEEN MORE GRATEFUL FOR THIS WEEK

I GIVE THIS WEEK A

SOMETHING I WANT TO REMEMBER ABOUT THIS WEEK

MY INTENTION FOR NEXT WEEK

SOMEONE I COULD HAVE FELT MORE GRATEFUL FOR THIS WEEK

DAY 211

DAY   MONTH   YEAR

THREE THINGS I'M GRATEFUL FOR

I GIVE TODAY A

SOMETHING I WANT TO REMEMBER ABOUT TODAY

SOMETHING I COULD HAVE BEEN MORE GRATEFUL FOR TODAY

MY INTENTION FOR TOMORROW

DAY 212

THREE THINGS I'M GRATEFUL FOR

SOMETHING I WANT TO REMEMBER ABOUT TODAY

I GIVE TODAY A

MY INTENTION FOR TOMORROW

SOMETHING I COULD HAVE BEEN MORE GRATEFUL FOR TODAY

DAY 213

DAY MONTH YEAR

THREE THINGS I'M GRATEFUL FOR

I GIVE TODAY A

SOMETHING I WANT TO REMEMBER ABOUT TODAY

SOMETHING I COULD HAVE BEEN MORE GRATEFUL FOR TODAY

MY INTENTION FOR
TOMORROW

DAY 214

THREE THINGS I'M GRATEFUL FOR

SOMETHING I WANT TO REMEMBER ABOUT TODAY

I GIVE TODAY A

MY INTENTION FOR TOMORROW

SOMETHING I COULD HAVE BEEN MORE GRATEFUL FOR TODAY

DAY 215

DAY   MONTH   YEAR

THREE THINGS I'M GRATEFUL FOR

I GIVE TODAY A   SOMETHING I WANT TO REMEMBER ABOUT TODAY

SOMETHING I COULD HAVE BEEN MORE GRATEFUL FOR TODAY   MY INTENTION FOR TOMORROW

DAY 216

THREE THINGS I'M GRATEFUL FOR

SOMETHING I WANT TO REMEMBER ABOUT TODAY

I GIVE TODAY A

MY INTENTION FOR TOMORROW

SOMETHING I COULD HAVE BEEN MORE GRATEFUL FOR TODAY

Day 217

Three things I'm grateful for

I GIVE TODAY A

SOMETHING I WANT TO REMEMBER ABOUT TODAY

SOMETHING I COULD HAVE BEEN MORE GRATEFUL FOR TODAY

MY INTENTION FOR TOMORROW

Day 217

Some people could be given an entire field of roses and only see the thorns in it. Others could be given a single weed and only see the wildflower in it. Perception is a key component to gratitude. And gratitude is a key component to joy.

Amy Weatherly

Something I could have been more grateful for this week

I give this week a

Something I want to remember about this week

My intention for next week

Someone I could have felt more grateful for this week

DAY 218

THREE THINGS I'M GRATEFUL FOR

I GIVE TODAY A

SOMETHING I WANT TO REMEMBER ABOUT TODAY

SOMETHING I COULD HAVE BEEN MORE GRATEFUL FOR TODAY

MY INTENTION FOR TOMORROW

DAY 219

DAY   MONTH   YEAR

THREE THINGS I'M GRATEFUL FOR

SOMETHING I WANT TO REMEMBER ABOUT TODAY   I GIVE TODAY A

MY INTENTION FOR   SOMETHING I COULD HAVE BEEN MORE GRATEFUL FOR TODAY
TOMORROW

Day 220

Day   Month   Year

Three things I'm grateful for

I give today a

Something I want to remember about today

Something I could have been more grateful for today

My intention for tomorrow

Day 221

Three things I'm grateful for

Something I want to remember about today

I give today a

My intention for
tomorrow

Something I could have been more grateful for today

DAY 222

DAY   MONTH   YEAR

THREE THINGS I'M GRATEFUL FOR

I GIVE TODAY A

SOMETHING I WANT TO REMEMBER ABOUT TODAY

SOMETHING I COULD HAVE BEEN MORE GRATEFUL FOR TODAY

MY INTENTION FOR
TOMORROW

DAY 223

DAY   MONTH   YEAR

THREE THINGS I'M GRATEFUL FOR

SOMETHING I WANT TO REMEMBER ABOUT TODAY

I GIVE TODAY A

MY INTENTION FOR TOMORROW

SOMETHING I COULD HAVE BEEN MORE GRATEFUL FOR TODAY

DAY 224

THREE THINGS I'M GRATEFUL FOR

I GIVE TODAY A

SOMETHING I WANT TO REMEMBER ABOUT TODAY

SOMETHING I COULD HAVE BEEN MORE GRATEFUL FOR TODAY

MY INTENTION FOR TOMORROW

DAY 224

LET US BE GRATEFUL TO THE PEOPLE WHO MAKE US HAPPY; THEY ARE THE CHARMING GARDENERS WHO MAKE OUR SOULS BLOSSOM.

Marcel Proust

SOMETHING I COULD HAVE BEEN MORE GRATEFUL FOR THESE PAST FOUR WEEKS

I GIVE THE PAST FOUR WEEKS A

SOMETHING I WANT TO REMEMBER ABOUT THE PAST FOUR WEEKS

MY INTENTION FOR THE NEXT FOUR WEEKS

SOMEONE I COULD HAVE FELT MORE GRATEFUL FOR THESE PAST FOUR WEEKS

DAY 225

DAY   MONTH   YEAR

THREE THINGS I'M GRATEFUL FOR

I GIVE TODAY A

SOMETHING I WANT TO REMEMBER ABOUT TODAY

SOMETHING I COULD HAVE BEEN MORE GRATEFUL FOR TODAY

MY INTENTION FOR TOMORROW

Day 226

Day   Month   Year

Three things I'm grateful for

Something I want to remember about today

I give today a

My intention for tomorrow

Something I could have been more grateful for today

Day 227

Day   Month   Year

Three things I'm grateful for

I give today a

Something I want to remember about today

Something I could have been more grateful for today

My intention for tomorrow

Day 228

Three things I'm grateful for

Something I want to remember about today

I give today a

My intention for
tomorrow

Something I could have been more grateful for today

DAY 229

DAY   MONTH   YEAR

THREE THINGS I'M GRATEFUL FOR

I GIVE TODAY A

SOMETHING I WANT TO REMEMBER ABOUT TODAY

SOMETHING I COULD HAVE BEEN MORE GRATEFUL FOR TODAY

MY INTENTION FOR TOMORROW

DAY 230

DAY   MONTH   YEAR

THREE THINGS I'M GRATEFUL FOR

SOMETHING I WANT TO REMEMBER ABOUT TODAY

I GIVE TODAY A

MY INTENTION FOR TOMORROW

SOMETHING I COULD HAVE BEEN MORE GRATEFUL FOR TODAY

DAY 231

DAY   MONTH   YEAR

THREE THINGS I'M GRATEFUL FOR

I GIVE TODAY A

SOMETHING I WANT TO REMEMBER ABOUT TODAY

SOMETHING I COULD HAVE BEEN MORE GRATEFUL FOR TODAY

MY INTENTION FOR TOMORROW

Day 231

Gratitude is riches, complaint is poverty.

Doris Day

Something I could have been more grateful for this week

I give this week a

Something I want to remember about this week

My intention for next week

Someone I could have felt more grateful for this week

DAY 232

DAY   MONTH   YEAR

THREE THINGS I'M GRATEFUL FOR

I GIVE TODAY A

SOMETHING I WANT TO REMEMBER ABOUT TODAY

SOMETHING I COULD HAVE BEEN MORE GRATEFUL FOR TODAY

MY INTENTION FOR
TOMORROW

Day 233

Three things I'm grateful for

Something I want to remember about today

I give today a

My intention for
tomorrow

Something I could have been more grateful for today

DAY 234

DAY   MONTH   YEAR

THREE THINGS I'M GRATEFUL FOR

I GIVE TODAY A

SOMETHING I WANT TO REMEMBER ABOUT TODAY

SOMETHING I COULD HAVE BEEN MORE GRATEFUL FOR TODAY

MY INTENTION FOR TOMORROW

Day 235

Day   Month   Year

Three things I'm grateful for

Something I want to remember about today   I give today a

My intention for   Something I could have been more grateful for today
tomorrow

DAY 236

DAY   MONTH   YEAR

THREE THINGS I'M GRATEFUL FOR

I GIVE TODAY A   SOMETHING I WANT TO REMEMBER ABOUT TODAY

SOMETHING I COULD HAVE BEEN MORE GRATEFUL FOR TODAY   MY INTENTION FOR
TOMORROW

DAY 237

THREE THINGS I'M GRATEFUL FOR

SOMETHING I WANT TO REMEMBER ABOUT TODAY

I GIVE TODAY A

MY INTENTION FOR
TOMORROW

SOMETHING I COULD HAVE BEEN MORE GRATEFUL FOR TODAY

DAY 238

THREE THINGS I'M GRATEFUL FOR

I GIVE TODAY A

SOMETHING I WANT TO REMEMBER ABOUT TODAY

SOMETHING I COULD HAVE BEEN MORE GRATEFUL FOR TODAY

MY INTENTION FOR
TOMORROW

DAY 238

How do you say 'Thank you' for sunshine or health...for clear days or gentle rains...
for happiness, joy or love? You say it by sharing what you have. You say it by making
the world a better place in which to live.
Thomas E. Willhite

Something I could have been more grateful for this week

I give this week a

Something I want to remember about this week

My intention for next week

Someone I could have felt more grateful for this week

DAY 239

THREE THINGS I'M GRATEFUL FOR

I GIVE TODAY A

SOMETHING I WANT TO REMEMBER ABOUT TODAY

SOMETHING I COULD HAVE BEEN MORE GRATEFUL FOR TODAY

MY INTENTION FOR TOMORROW

Day 240

Three things I'm grateful for

Something I want to remember about today

I give today a

My intention for tomorrow

Something I could have been more grateful for today

Day 241

Day   Month   Year

Three things I'm grateful for

I give today a

Something I want to remember about today

Something I could have been more grateful for today

My intention for
tomorrow

DAY 242

DAY   MONTH   YEAR

THREE THINGS I'M GRATEFUL FOR

SOMETHING I WANT TO REMEMBER ABOUT TODAY

I GIVE TODAY A

MY INTENTION FOR
TOMORROW

SOMETHING I COULD HAVE BEEN MORE GRATEFUL FOR TODAY

DAY 243

Day   Month   Year

Three things I'm grateful for

I give today a   Something I want to remember about today

Something I could have been more grateful for today   My intention for tomorrow

DAY 244

THREE THINGS I'M GRATEFUL FOR

SOMETHING I WANT TO REMEMBER ABOUT TODAY

I GIVE TODAY A

MY INTENTION FOR TOMORROW

SOMETHING I COULD HAVE BEEN MORE GRATEFUL FOR TODAY

Day 245

Day   Month   Year

Three things I'm grateful for

I give today a

Something I want to remember about today

Something I could have been more grateful for today

My intention for tomorrow

Day 245

Gratitude is the direct way out of comparison.

Robyn Conley Downs

Something I could have been more grateful for this week

I give this week a

Something I want to remember about this week

My intention for next week

Someone I could have felt more grateful for this week

DAY 246

DAY   MONTH   YEAR

THREE THINGS I'M GRATEFUL FOR

I GIVE TODAY A   SOMETHING I WANT TO REMEMBER ABOUT TODAY

SOMETHING I COULD HAVE BEEN MORE GRATEFUL FOR TODAY   MY INTENTION FOR
TOMORROW

Day 247

Three things I'm grateful for

Something I want to remember about today

I give today a

My intention for
tomorrow

Something I could have been more grateful for today

DAY 248

DAY   MONTH   YEAR

THREE THINGS I'M GRATEFUL FOR

I GIVE TODAY A

SOMETHING I WANT TO REMEMBER ABOUT TODAY

SOMETHING I COULD HAVE BEEN MORE GRATEFUL FOR TODAY

MY INTENTION FOR TOMORROW

Day 249

Three things I'm grateful for

Something I want to remember about today   I give today a

My intention for   Something I could have been more grateful for today
tomorrow

DAY 250

DAY   MONTH   YEAR

THREE THINGS I'M GRATEFUL FOR

I GIVE TODAY A   SOMETHING I WANT TO REMEMBER ABOUT TODAY

SOMETHING I COULD HAVE BEEN MORE GRATEFUL FOR TODAY   MY INTENTION FOR TOMORROW

Day 251

Three things I'm grateful for

Something I want to remember about today

I give today a

My intention for
tomorrow

Something I could have been more grateful for today

DAY 252

DAY   MONTH   YEAR

THREE THINGS I'M GRATEFUL FOR

I GIVE TODAY A

SOMETHING I WANT TO REMEMBER ABOUT TODAY

SOMETHING I COULD HAVE BEEN MORE GRATEFUL FOR TODAY

MY INTENTION FOR
TOMORROW

DAY 252

The simple things are also the most extraordinary things, and only the wise can see them.

Paulo Coelho

Something I could have been more grateful for these past four weeks

I give the past four weeks a

Something I want to remember about the past four weeks

My intention for the next four weeks

Someone I could have felt more grateful for these past four weeks

DAY 253

DAY   MONTH   YEAR

THREE THINGS I'M GRATEFUL FOR

I GIVE TODAY A

SOMETHING I WANT TO REMEMBER ABOUT TODAY

SOMETHING I COULD HAVE BEEN MORE GRATEFUL FOR TODAY

MY INTENTION FOR TOMORROW

Day 254

Three things I'm grateful for

Something I want to remember about today

I give today a

My intention for tomorrow

Something I could have been more grateful for today

DAY 255

DAY   MONTH   YEAR

THREE THINGS I'M GRATEFUL FOR

I GIVE TODAY A

SOMETHING I WANT TO REMEMBER ABOUT TODAY

SOMETHING I COULD HAVE BEEN MORE GRATEFUL FOR TODAY

MY INTENTION FOR TOMORROW

DAY 256

Day   Month   Year

Three things I'm grateful for

Something I want to remember about today   I give today a

My intention for
tomorrow   Something I could have been more grateful for today

DAY 257

DAY MONTH YEAR

THREE THINGS I'M GRATEFUL FOR

I GIVE TODAY A

SOMETHING I WANT TO REMEMBER ABOUT TODAY

SOMETHING I COULD HAVE BEEN MORE GRATEFUL FOR TODAY

MY INTENTION FOR
TOMORROW

Day 258

Day   Month   Year

Three things I'm grateful for

Something I want to remember about today

I give today a

My intention for tomorrow

Something I could have been more grateful for today

DAY 259

DAY   MONTH   YEAR

THREE THINGS I'M GRATEFUL FOR

I GIVE TODAY A   SOMETHING I WANT TO REMEMBER ABOUT TODAY

SOMETHING I COULD HAVE BEEN MORE GRATEFUL FOR TODAY   MY INTENTION FOR TOMORROW

DAY 259

INHALE LOVE, EXHALE GRATITUDE

Unknown

SOMETHING I COULD HAVE BEEN MORE GRATEFUL FOR THIS WEEK

I GIVE THIS WEEK A

SOMETHING I WANT TO REMEMBER ABOUT THIS WEEK

MY INTENTION FOR NEXT WEEK

SOMEONE I COULD HAVE FELT MORE GRATEFUL FOR THIS WEEK

DAY 260

DAY   MONTH   YEAR

THREE THINGS I'M GRATEFUL FOR

I GIVE TODAY A

SOMETHING I WANT TO REMEMBER ABOUT TODAY

SOMETHING I COULD HAVE BEEN MORE GRATEFUL FOR TODAY

MY INTENTION FOR
TOMORROW

DAY 261

<table>
<tr><td>DAY</td><td>MONTH</td><td>YEAR</td></tr>
</table>

THREE THINGS I'M GRATEFUL FOR

SOMETHING I WANT TO REMEMBER ABOUT TODAY

I GIVE TODAY A

MY INTENTION FOR TOMORROW

SOMETHING I COULD HAVE BEEN MORE GRATEFUL FOR TODAY

DAY 262

DAY   MONTH   YEAR

THREE THINGS I'M GRATEFUL FOR

I GIVE TODAY A

SOMETHING I WANT TO REMEMBER ABOUT TODAY

SOMETHING I COULD HAVE BEEN MORE GRATEFUL FOR TODAY

MY INTENTION FOR TOMORROW

Day 263

Day

Month

Year

Three things I'm grateful for

Something I want to remember about today

I give today a

My intention for
tomorrow

Something I could have been more grateful for today

DAY 264

DAY   MONTH   YEAR

THREE THINGS I'M GRATEFUL FOR

I GIVE TODAY A

SOMETHING I WANT TO REMEMBER ABOUT TODAY

SOMETHING I COULD HAVE BEEN MORE GRATEFUL FOR TODAY

MY INTENTION FOR TOMORROW

DAY 265

DAY   MONTH   YEAR

THREE THINGS I'M GRATEFUL FOR

SOMETHING I WANT TO REMEMBER ABOUT TODAY

I GIVE TODAY A

MY INTENTION FOR
TOMORROW

SOMETHING I COULD HAVE BEEN MORE GRATEFUL FOR TODAY

DAY 266

<table>
<tr><td>DAY</td><td>MONTH</td><td>YEAR</td></tr>
</table>

THREE THINGS I'M GRATEFUL FOR

I GIVE TODAY A

SOMETHING I WANT TO REMEMBER ABOUT TODAY

SOMETHING I COULD HAVE BEEN MORE GRATEFUL FOR TODAY

MY INTENTION FOR TOMORROW

WHEN GRATITUDE REPLACES JUDGMENT, PEACE SPREADS THROUGHOUT BODY, GENTLENESS EMBRACES YOUR SOUL, WISDOM FILLS THE MIND.

Neale Donald Walsch

SOMETHING I COULD HAVE BEEN MORE GRATEFUL FOR THIS WEEK

I GIVE THIS WEEK A

SOMETHING I WANT TO REMEMBER ABOUT THIS WEEK

MY INTENTION FOR NEXT WEEK

SOMEONE I COULD HAVE FELT MORE GRATEFUL FOR THIS WEEK

DAY 267

DAY   MONTH   YEAR

THREE THINGS I'M GRATEFUL FOR

I GIVE TODAY A

SOMETHING I WANT TO REMEMBER ABOUT TODAY

SOMETHING I COULD HAVE BEEN MORE GRATEFUL FOR TODAY

MY INTENTION FOR
TOMORROW

Day 268

Day   Month   Year

Three things I'm grateful for

Something I want to remember about today

I give today a

My intention for tomorrow

Something I could have been more grateful for today

DAY 269

DAY   MONTH   YEAR

THREE THINGS I'M GRATEFUL FOR

I GIVE TODAY A

SOMETHING I WANT TO REMEMBER ABOUT TODAY

SOMETHING I COULD HAVE BEEN MORE GRATEFUL FOR TODAY

MY INTENTION FOR TOMORROW

Day 270

Day   Month   Year

Three things I'm grateful for

Something I want to remember about today   I give today a

My intention for   Something I could have been more grateful for today
tomorrow

DAY 271

THREE THINGS I'M GRATEFUL FOR

I GIVE TODAY A

SOMETHING I WANT TO REMEMBER ABOUT TODAY

SOMETHING I COULD HAVE BEEN MORE GRATEFUL FOR TODAY

MY INTENTION FOR TOMORROW

Day 272

Three things I'm grateful for

Something I want to remember about today

I give today a

My intention for tomorrow

Something I could have been more grateful for today

DAY 273

THREE THINGS I'M GRATEFUL FOR

I GIVE TODAY A

SOMETHING I WANT TO REMEMBER ABOUT TODAY

SOMETHING I COULD HAVE BEEN MORE GRATEFUL FOR TODAY

MY INTENTION FOR
TOMORROW

Day 273

You have a choice each and every single day. I choose to feel blessed.
I choose to feel grateful. I choose to be excited. I choose to be thankful.
I choose to be happy.

Amber Housley

Something I could have been more grateful for this week

I give this week a

Something I want to remember about this week

My intention for next week

Someone I could have felt more grateful for this week

9 MONTHS

Let's do some more reflecting. Run through the past thirteen weeks and answer the following:

SOMETHING I WANT TO REMEMBER ABOUT THE PAST THREE MONTHS

LOOKING BACK OVER THE PAST THREE MONTHS, I AM MOST GRATEFUL FOR

THE BIGGEST LESSON I LEARNED OVER THE PAST THREE MONTHS

SOMEONE OR SOMETHING I COULD HAVE FELT MORE GRATEFUL FOR DURING THE PAST THREE MONTHS

9 MONTHS

WHAT HAVE I BEEN UNABLE TO FEEL GRATEFUL FOR DURING THE PAST THREE MONTHS? CAN I REFORMULATE THAT THOUGHT ANYWAY?

I AM GRATEFUL...

WHEN LOOKING BACK ON HOW I'VE RATED MY WEEKS THUS FAR, THE NUMBERS TELL ME

MY INTENTION FOR THE NEXT THREE MONTHS

WHO HAVE I BEEN UNABLE TO FEEL GRATEFUL FOR DURING THE PAST THREE MONTHS? CAN I REFORMULATE THAT THOUGHT ANYWAY? I AM GRATEFUL...

DAY 274

DAY   MONTH   YEAR

THREE THINGS I'M GRATEFUL FOR

I GIVE TODAY A   SOMETHING I WANT TO REMEMBER ABOUT TODAY

SOMETHING I COULD HAVE BEEN MORE GRATEFUL FOR TODAY   MY INTENTION FOR
TOMORROW

DAY 275

THREE THINGS I'M GRATEFUL FOR

SOMETHING I WANT TO REMEMBER ABOUT TODAY

I GIVE TODAY A

MY INTENTION FOR
TOMORROW

SOMETHING I COULD HAVE BEEN MORE GRATEFUL FOR TODAY

DAY 276

DAY MONTH YEAR

THREE THINGS I'M GRATEFUL FOR

I GIVE TODAY A

SOMETHING I WANT TO REMEMBER ABOUT TODAY

SOMETHING I COULD HAVE BEEN MORE GRATEFUL FOR TODAY

MY INTENTION FOR TOMORROW

Day 277

Day   Month   Year

Three things I'm grateful for

Something I want to remember about today

I give today a

My intention for tomorrow

Something I could have been more grateful for today

DAY 278

DAY   MONTH   YEAR

THREE THINGS I'M GRATEFUL FOR

I GIVE TODAY A   SOMETHING I WANT TO REMEMBER ABOUT TODAY

SOMETHING I COULD HAVE BEEN MORE GRATEFUL FOR TODAY   MY INTENTION FOR
                                                             TOMORROW

DAY 279

DAY   MONTH   YEAR

THREE THINGS I'M GRATEFUL FOR

SOMETHING I WANT TO REMEMBER ABOUT TODAY

I GIVE TODAY A

MY INTENTION FOR
TOMORROW

SOMETHING I COULD HAVE BEEN MORE GRATEFUL FOR TODAY

DAY 280

DAY   MONTH   YEAR

THREE THINGS I'M GRATEFUL FOR

I GIVE TODAY A   SOMETHING I WANT TO REMEMBER ABOUT TODAY

SOMETHING I COULD HAVE BEEN MORE GRATEFUL FOR TODAY   MY INTENTION FOR TOMORROW

THANKFULNESS IS THE QUICKEST PATH TO JOY.

Jefferson Bethke

SOMETHING I COULD HAVE BEEN MORE GRATEFUL FOR THESE PAST FOUR WEEKS

I GIVE THE PAST FOUR WEEKS A

SOMETHING I WANT TO REMEMBER ABOUT THE PAST FOUR WEEKS

MY INTENTION FOR THE NEXT FOUR WEEKS

SOMEONE I COULD HAVE FELT MORE GRATEFUL FOR THESE PAST FOUR WEEKS

DAY 281

DAY   MONTH   YEAR

THREE THINGS I'M GRATEFUL FOR

I GIVE TODAY A

SOMETHING I WANT TO REMEMBER ABOUT TODAY

SOMETHING I COULD HAVE BEEN MORE GRATEFUL FOR TODAY

MY INTENTION FOR
TOMORROW

DAY 282

THREE THINGS I'M GRATEFUL FOR

SOMETHING I WANT TO REMEMBER ABOUT TODAY

I GIVE TODAY A

MY INTENTION FOR
TOMORROW

SOMETHING I COULD HAVE BEEN MORE GRATEFUL FOR TODAY

DAY 283

DAY   MONTH   YEAR

Three things I'm grateful for

I GIVE TODAY A

SOMETHING I WANT TO REMEMBER ABOUT TODAY

SOMETHING I COULD HAVE BEEN MORE GRATEFUL FOR TODAY

MY INTENTION FOR TOMORROW

Day 284

Day   Month   Year

Three things I'm grateful for

Something I want to remember about today

I give today a

My intention for tomorrow

Something I could have been more grateful for today

DAY 285

DAY   MONTH   YEAR

THREE THINGS I'M GRATEFUL FOR

I GIVE TODAY A

SOMETHING I WANT TO REMEMBER ABOUT TODAY

SOMETHING I COULD HAVE BEEN MORE GRATEFUL FOR TODAY

MY INTENTION FOR
TOMORROW

DAY 286

Day   Month   Year

Three things I'm grateful for

Something I want to remember about today   I give today a

My intention for   Something I could have been more grateful for today
tomorrow

DAY 287

DAY   MONTH   YEAR

THREE THINGS I'M GRATEFUL FOR

I GIVE TODAY A

SOMETHING I WANT TO REMEMBER ABOUT TODAY

SOMETHING I COULD HAVE BEEN MORE GRATEFUL FOR TODAY

MY INTENTION FOR TOMORROW

DAY 287

Gratitude should not be just a reaction to getting what you want but an all-the-time gratitude, the kind where you notice the little things and where you constantly look for the good, even in unpleasant situations. Start bringing gratitude to your experiences, instead of waiting for a positive experience in order to feel grateful.

Marelisa Fábrega

Something I could have been more grateful for this week

I give this week a

Something I want to remember about this week

My intention for next week

Someone I could have felt more grateful for this week

DAY 288

DAY   MONTH   YEAR

THREE THINGS I'M GRATEFUL FOR

I GIVE TODAY A

SOMETHING I WANT TO REMEMBER ABOUT TODAY

SOMETHING I COULD HAVE BEEN MORE GRATEFUL FOR TODAY

MY INTENTION FOR
TOMORROW

Day 289

Day   Month   Year

Three things I'm grateful for

Something I want to remember about today   I give today a

My intention for   Something I could have been more grateful for today
tomorrow

DAY 290

DAY   MONTH   YEAR

THREE THINGS I'M GRATEFUL FOR

I GIVE TODAY A

SOMETHING I WANT TO REMEMBER ABOUT TODAY

SOMETHING I COULD HAVE BEEN MORE GRATEFUL FOR TODAY

MY INTENTION FOR TOMORROW

Day 291

Day   Month   Year

Three things I'm grateful for

Something I want to remember about today

I give today a

My intention for
tomorrow

Something I could have been more grateful for today

DAY 292

DAY   MONTH   YEAR

THREE THINGS I'M GRATEFUL FOR

I GIVE TODAY A   SOMETHING I WANT TO REMEMBER ABOUT TODAY

SOMETHING I COULD HAVE BEEN MORE GRATEFUL FOR TODAY   MY INTENTION FOR TOMORROW

Day 293

Three things I'm grateful for

Something I want to remember about today

I give today a

My intention for
tomorrow

Something I could have been more grateful for today

DAY 294

DAY   MONTH   YEAR

THREE THINGS I'M GRATEFUL FOR

I GIVE TODAY A

SOMETHING I WANT TO REMEMBER ABOUT TODAY

SOMETHING I COULD HAVE BEEN MORE GRATEFUL FOR TODAY

MY INTENTION FOR TOMORROW

DAY 294

A GRATEFUL MIND IS A GREAT MIND WHICH EVENTUALLY ATTRACTS TO ITSELF GREAT THINGS.

PLATO

SOMETHING I COULD HAVE BEEN MORE GRATEFUL FOR THIS WEEK

I GIVE THIS WEEK A

SOMETHING I WANT TO REMEMBER ABOUT THIS WEEK

MY INTENTION FOR NEXT WEEK

SOMEONE I COULD HAVE FELT MORE GRATEFUL FOR THIS WEEK

DAY 295

DAY   MONTH   YEAR

THREE THINGS I'M GRATEFUL FOR

I GIVE TODAY A

SOMETHING I WANT TO REMEMBER ABOUT TODAY

SOMETHING I COULD HAVE BEEN MORE GRATEFUL FOR TODAY

MY INTENTION FOR
TOMORROW

Day 296

Day   Month   Year

Three things I'm grateful for

Something I want to remember about today

I give today a

My intention for tomorrow

Something I could have been more grateful for today

DAY 297

DAY   MONTH   YEAR

THREE THINGS I'M GRATEFUL FOR

I GIVE TODAY A

SOMETHING I WANT TO REMEMBER ABOUT TODAY

SOMETHING I COULD HAVE BEEN MORE GRATEFUL FOR TODAY

MY INTENTION FOR TOMORROW

DAY 298

Day   Month   Year

Three things I'm grateful for

Something I want to remember about today   I give today a

My intention for   Something I could have been more grateful for today
tomorrow

DAY 299

DAY   MONTH   YEAR

THREE THINGS I'M GRATEFUL FOR

I GIVE TODAY A

SOMETHING I WANT TO REMEMBER ABOUT TODAY

SOMETHING I COULD HAVE BEEN MORE GRATEFUL FOR TODAY

MY INTENTION FOR TOMORROW

DAY 300

DAY   MONTH   YEAR

THREE THINGS I'M GRATEFUL FOR

SOMETHING I WANT TO REMEMBER ABOUT TODAY

I GIVE TODAY A

MY INTENTION FOR TOMORROW

SOMETHING I COULD HAVE BEEN MORE GRATEFUL FOR TODAY

DAY 301

DAY　　　　　MONTH　　　　　YEAR

THREE THINGS I'M GRATEFUL FOR

I GIVE TODAY A

SOMETHING I WANT TO REMEMBER ABOUT TODAY

SOMETHING I COULD HAVE BEEN MORE GRATEFUL FOR TODAY

MY INTENTION FOR TOMORROW

DAY 301

A GRATEFUL HEART IS A MAGNET FOR MIRACLES.

UNKNOWN

SOMETHING I COULD HAVE BEEN MORE GRATEFUL FOR THIS WEEK

I GIVE THIS WEEK A

SOMETHING I WANT TO REMEMBER ABOUT THIS WEEK

MY INTENTION FOR NEXT WEEK

SOMEONE I COULD HAVE FELT MORE GRATEFUL FOR THIS WEEK

DAY 302

DAY   MONTH   YEAR

THREE THINGS I'M GRATEFUL FOR

I GIVE TODAY A

SOMETHING I WANT TO REMEMBER ABOUT TODAY

SOMETHING I COULD HAVE BEEN MORE GRATEFUL FOR TODAY

MY INTENTION FOR TOMORROW

DAY 303

THREE THINGS I'M GRATEFUL FOR

SOMETHING I WANT TO REMEMBER ABOUT TODAY

I GIVE TODAY A

MY INTENTION FOR TOMORROW

SOMETHING I COULD HAVE BEEN MORE GRATEFUL FOR TODAY

DAY 304

Three things I'm grateful for

I GIVE TODAY A

SOMETHING I WANT TO REMEMBER ABOUT TODAY

SOMETHING I COULD HAVE BEEN MORE GRATEFUL FOR TODAY

MY INTENTION FOR TOMORROW

DAY 305

Day   Month   Year

Three things I'm grateful for

Something I want to remember about today   I give today a

My intention for
tomorrow   Something I could have been more grateful for today

DAY 306

THREE THINGS I'M GRATEFUL FOR

I GIVE TODAY A

SOMETHING I WANT TO REMEMBER ABOUT TODAY

SOMETHING I COULD HAVE BEEN MORE GRATEFUL FOR TODAY

MY INTENTION FOR TOMORROW

DAY 307

THREE THINGS I'M GRATEFUL FOR

SOMETHING I WANT TO REMEMBER ABOUT TODAY

I GIVE TODAY A

MY INTENTION FOR TOMORROW

SOMETHING I COULD HAVE BEEN MORE GRATEFUL FOR TODAY

DAY 308

THREE THINGS I'M GRATEFUL FOR

I GIVE TODAY A   SOMETHING I WANT TO REMEMBER ABOUT TODAY

SOMETHING I COULD HAVE BEEN MORE GRATEFUL FOR TODAY   MY INTENTION FOR
                                                                            TOMORROW

DAY 308

I WOKE TODAY WITH GRATITUDE FOR THOSE WHO SHARE ME IN THEIR LIVES. I AM THANKFUL FOR THOSE WHO ARE PART OF MY JOURNEY.

Millie Mestril

SOMETHING I COULD HAVE BEEN MORE GRATEFUL FOR THESE PAST FOUR WEEKS

I GIVE THE PAST FOUR WEEKS A

SOMETHING I WANT TO REMEMBER ABOUT THE PAST FOUR WEEKS

MY INTENTION FOR THE NEXT FOUR WEEKS

SOMEONE I COULD HAVE FELT MORE GRATEFUL FOR THESE PAST FOUR WEEKS

DAY 309

THREE THINGS I'M GRATEFUL FOR

I GIVE TODAY A

SOMETHING I WANT TO REMEMBER ABOUT TODAY

SOMETHING I COULD HAVE BEEN MORE GRATEFUL FOR TODAY

MY INTENTION FOR TOMORROW

DAY 310

Day　　　　　Month　　　　　Year

Three things I'm grateful for

Something I want to remember about today　　　　　　　　　　I give today a

My intention for
tomorrow　　　　　　　Something I could have been more grateful for today

DAY 311

DAY   MONTH   YEAR

THREE THINGS I'M GRATEFUL FOR

I GIVE TODAY A   SOMETHING I WANT TO REMEMBER ABOUT TODAY

SOMETHING I COULD HAVE BEEN MORE GRATEFUL FOR TODAY   MY INTENTION FOR
                                                                       TOMORROW

DAY 312

THREE THINGS I'M GRATEFUL FOR

SOMETHING I WANT TO REMEMBER ABOUT TODAY

I GIVE TODAY A

MY INTENTION FOR
TOMORROW

SOMETHING I COULD HAVE BEEN MORE GRATEFUL FOR TODAY

DAY 313

DAY   MONTH   YEAR

THREE THINGS I'M GRATEFUL FOR

I GIVE TODAY A   SOMETHING I WANT TO REMEMBER ABOUT TODAY

SOMETHING I COULD HAVE BEEN MORE GRATEFUL FOR TODAY   MY INTENTION FOR
TOMORROW

DAY 314

DAY   MONTH   YEAR

THREE THINGS I'M GRATEFUL FOR

SOMETHING I WANT TO REMEMBER ABOUT TODAY

I GIVE TODAY A

MY INTENTION FOR
TOMORROW

SOMETHING I COULD HAVE BEEN MORE GRATEFUL FOR TODAY

DAY 315

DAY   MONTH   YEAR

THREE THINGS I'M GRATEFUL FOR

I GIVE TODAY A   SOMETHING I WANT TO REMEMBER ABOUT TODAY

SOMETHING I COULD HAVE BEEN MORE GRATEFUL FOR TODAY   MY INTENTION FOR
TOMORROW

DAY 315

YOUR MANTRA IS THANK YOU. JUST KEEP SAYING THANK YOU. DON'T EXPLAIN. DON'T COMPLAIN. JUST SAY THANK YOU. SAY THANK YOU TO EXISTENCE.

MOOJI

SOMETHING I COULD HAVE BEEN MORE GRATEFUL FOR THIS WEEK

I GIVE THIS WEEK A

SOMETHING I WANT TO REMEMBER ABOUT THIS WEEK

MY INTENTION FOR NEXT WEEK

SOMEONE I COULD HAVE FELT MORE GRATEFUL FOR THIS WEEK

DAY 316

DAY   MONTH   YEAR

THREE THINGS I'M GRATEFUL FOR

I GIVE TODAY A

SOMETHING I WANT TO REMEMBER ABOUT TODAY

SOMETHING I COULD HAVE BEEN MORE GRATEFUL FOR TODAY

MY INTENTION FOR TOMORROW

Day 317

Three things I'm grateful for

Something I want to remember about today

I give today a

My intention for tomorrow

Something I could have been more grateful for today

DAY 318

Three things I'm grateful for

I give today a

Something I want to remember about today

Something I could have been more grateful for today

My intention for tomorrow

DAY 319

DAY   MONTH   YEAR

THREE THINGS I'M GRATEFUL FOR

SOMETHING I WANT TO REMEMBER ABOUT TODAY

I GIVE TODAY A

MY INTENTION FOR TOMORROW

SOMETHING I COULD HAVE BEEN MORE GRATEFUL FOR TODAY

DAY 320

<table>
<tr><td>DAY</td><td>MONTH</td><td>YEAR</td></tr>
</table>

THREE THINGS I'M GRATEFUL FOR

I GIVE TODAY A

SOMETHING I WANT TO REMEMBER ABOUT TODAY

SOMETHING I COULD HAVE BEEN MORE GRATEFUL FOR TODAY

MY INTENTION FOR TOMORROW

Day 321

Day   Month   Year

Three things I'm grateful for

Something I want to remember about today

I give today a

My intention for tomorrow

Something I could have been more grateful for today

DAY 322

DAY   MONTH   YEAR

THREE THINGS I'M GRATEFUL FOR

I GIVE TODAY A

SOMETHING I WANT TO REMEMBER ABOUT TODAY

SOMETHING I COULD HAVE BEEN MORE GRATEFUL FOR TODAY

MY INTENTION FOR TOMORROW

DAY 322

GRATITUDE GENTLES EVEN THE ROUGHEST ROADS AND GIVES WINGS TO THE HEART.

Sue Patton Thoele

Something I could have been more grateful for this week

I give this week a

Something I want to remember about this week

My intention for next week

Someone I could have felt more grateful for this week

DAY 323

Day   Month   Year

Three things I'm grateful for

I give today a

Something I want to remember about today

Something I could have been more grateful for today

My intention for tomorrow

DAY 324

Day   Month   Year

Three things I'm grateful for

Something I want to remember about today   I give today a

My intention for   Something I could have been more grateful for today
tomorrow

Day 325

Day   Month   Year

Three things I'm grateful for

I give today a

Something I want to remember about today

Something I could have been more grateful for today

My intention for tomorrow

DAY 326

Three things I'm grateful for

Something I want to remember about today

I give today a

My intention for
tomorrow

Something I could have been more grateful for today

DAY 327

THREE THINGS I'M GRATEFUL FOR

I GIVE TODAY A

SOMETHING I WANT TO REMEMBER ABOUT TODAY

SOMETHING I COULD HAVE BEEN MORE GRATEFUL FOR TODAY

MY INTENTION FOR
TOMORROW

DAY   MONTH   YEAR

THREE THINGS I'M GRATEFUL FOR

SOMETHING I WANT TO REMEMBER ABOUT TODAY   I GIVE TODAY A

MY INTENTION FOR
TOMORROW   SOMETHING I COULD HAVE BEEN MORE GRATEFUL FOR TODAY

DAY 329

DAY   MONTH   YEAR

THREE THINGS I'M GRATEFUL FOR

I GIVE TODAY A   SOMETHING I WANT TO REMEMBER ABOUT TODAY

SOMETHING I COULD HAVE BEEN MORE GRATEFUL FOR TODAY   MY INTENTION FOR TOMORROW

DAY 329

WHEN YOU FOCUS ON THE GOOD,
THE GOOD GETS BETTER.

ABRAHAM HICKS

SOMETHING I COULD HAVE BEEN MORE GRATEFUL FOR THIS WEEK

I GIVE THIS WEEK A

SOMETHING I WANT TO REMEMBER ABOUT THIS WEEK

MY INTENTION FOR NEXT WEEK

SOMEONE I COULD HAVE FELT MORE GRATEFUL FOR THIS WEEK

DAY 330

DAY   MONTH   YEAR

THREE THINGS I'M GRATEFUL FOR

I GIVE TODAY A

SOMETHING I WANT TO REMEMBER ABOUT TODAY

SOMETHING I COULD HAVE BEEN MORE GRATEFUL FOR TODAY

MY INTENTION FOR TOMORROW

DAY 331

THREE THINGS I'M GRATEFUL FOR

SOMETHING I WANT TO REMEMBER ABOUT TODAY

I GIVE TODAY A

MY INTENTION FOR TOMORROW

SOMETHING I COULD HAVE BEEN MORE GRATEFUL FOR TODAY

DAY 332

DAY   MONTH   YEAR

THREE THINGS I'M GRATEFUL FOR

I GIVE TODAY A

SOMETHING I WANT TO REMEMBER ABOUT TODAY

SOMETHING I COULD HAVE BEEN MORE GRATEFUL FOR TODAY

MY INTENTION FOR TOMORROW

Day 333

Day   Month   Year

Three things I'm grateful for

Something I want to remember about today

I give today a

My intention for tomorrow

Something I could have been more grateful for today

DAY 334

DAY   MONTH   YEAR

THREE THINGS I'M GRATEFUL FOR

I GIVE TODAY A   SOMETHING I WANT TO REMEMBER ABOUT TODAY

SOMETHING I COULD HAVE BEEN MORE GRATEFUL FOR TODAY   MY INTENTION FOR TOMORROW

DAY 335

THREE THINGS I'M GRATEFUL FOR

SOMETHING I WANT TO REMEMBER ABOUT TODAY

I GIVE TODAY A

MY INTENTION FOR
TOMORROW

SOMETHING I COULD HAVE BEEN MORE GRATEFUL FOR TODAY

DAY 336

DAY   MONTH   YEAR

THREE THINGS I'M GRATEFUL FOR

I GIVE TODAY A

SOMETHING I WANT TO REMEMBER ABOUT TODAY

SOMETHING I COULD HAVE BEEN MORE GRATEFUL FOR TODAY

MY INTENTION FOR TOMORROW

THE MOST BEAUTIFUL WAY TO START AND END THE DAY IS WITH A GRATEFUL HEART.

UNKNOWN

SOMETHING I COULD HAVE BEEN MORE GRATEFUL FOR THESE PAST FOUR WEEKS

I GIVE THE PAST FOUR WEEKS A 

SOMETHING I WANT TO REMEMBER ABOUT THE PAST FOUR WEEKS

MY INTENTION FOR THE NEXT FOUR WEEKS

SOMEONE I COULD HAVE FELT MORE GRATEFUL FOR THESE PAST FOUR WEEKS

DAY 337

THREE THINGS I'M GRATEFUL FOR

I GIVE TODAY A

SOMETHING I WANT TO REMEMBER ABOUT TODAY

SOMETHING I COULD HAVE BEEN MORE GRATEFUL FOR TODAY

MY INTENTION FOR
TOMORROW

Day 338

Three things I'm grateful for

Something I want to remember about today

I give today a

My intention for tomorrow

Something I could have been more grateful for today

DAY 339

DAY   MONTH   YEAR

THREE THINGS I'M GRATEFUL FOR

I GIVE TODAY A

SOMETHING I WANT TO REMEMBER ABOUT TODAY

SOMETHING I COULD HAVE BEEN MORE GRATEFUL FOR TODAY

MY INTENTION FOR TOMORROW

Day 340

Day   Month   Year

Three things I'm grateful for

Something I want to remember about today

I give today a

My intention for
tomorrow

Something I could have been more grateful for today

DAY 341

DAY   MONTH   YEAR

THREE THINGS I'M GRATEFUL FOR

I GIVE TODAY A

SOMETHING I WANT TO REMEMBER ABOUT TODAY

SOMETHING I COULD HAVE BEEN MORE GRATEFUL FOR TODAY

MY INTENTION FOR
TOMORROW

DAY 342

THREE THINGS I'M GRATEFUL FOR

SOMETHING I WANT TO REMEMBER ABOUT TODAY

I GIVE TODAY A

MY INTENTION FOR
TOMORROW

SOMETHING I COULD HAVE BEEN MORE GRATEFUL FOR TODAY

DAY 343

THREE THINGS I'M GRATEFUL FOR

I GIVE TODAY A

SOMETHING I WANT TO REMEMBER ABOUT TODAY

SOMETHING I COULD HAVE BEEN MORE GRATEFUL FOR TODAY

MY INTENTION FOR TOMORROW

Day 343

Gratitude helps you fall in love with the life you already have.

Kristen Hewitt

Something I could have been more grateful for this week

I give this week a

Something I want to remember about this week

My intention for next week

Someone I could have felt more grateful for this week

DAY 344

DAY   MONTH   YEAR

THREE THINGS I'M GRATEFUL FOR

I GIVE TODAY A

SOMETHING I WANT TO REMEMBER ABOUT TODAY

SOMETHING I COULD HAVE BEEN MORE GRATEFUL FOR TODAY

MY INTENTION FOR TOMORROW

DAY 345

DAY   MONTH   YEAR

THREE THINGS I'M GRATEFUL FOR

SOMETHING I WANT TO REMEMBER ABOUT TODAY

I GIVE TODAY A

MY INTENTION FOR TOMORROW

SOMETHINC I COULD HAVE BEEN MORE GRATEFUL FOR TODAY

DAY 346

Day   Month   Year

Three things I'm grateful for

I give today a

Something I want to remember about today

Something I could have been more grateful for today

My intention for tomorrow

Day 347

Day   Month   Year

Three things I'm grateful for

Something I want to remember about today   I give today a

My intention for   Something I could have been more grateful for today
tomorrow

DAY 348

DAY   MONTH   YEAR

THREE THINGS I'M GRATEFUL FOR

I GIVE TODAY A   SOMETHING I WANT TO REMEMBER ABOUT TODAY

SOMETHING I COULD HAVE BEEN MORE GRATEFUL FOR TODAY   MY INTENTION FOR TOMORROW

Day 349

Day   Month   Year

Three things I'm grateful for

Something I want to remember about today   I give today a

My intention for   Something I could have been more grateful for today
tomorrow

DAY 350

Three things I'm grateful for

I give today a

Something I want to remember about today

Something I could have been more grateful for today

My intention for tomorrow

DAY 350

Some people grumble that roses have thorns; I am grateful that thorns have roses.

Alphonse Karr

Something I could have been more grateful for this week

I give this week a

Something I want to remember about this week

My intention for next week

Someone I could have felt more grateful for this week

DAY 351

DAY   MONTH   YEAR

THREE THINGS I'M GRATEFUL FOR

I GIVE TODAY A   SOMETHING I WANT TO REMEMBER ABOUT TODAY

SOMETHING I COULD HAVE BEEN MORE GRATEFUL FOR TODAY   MY INTENTION FOR
TOMORROW

DAY 352

Day   Month   Year

Three things I'm grateful for

Something I want to remember about today

I give today a

My intention for tomorrow

Something I could have been more grateful for today

DAY 353

DAY   MONTH   YEAR

THREE THINGS I'M GRATEFUL FOR

I GIVE TODAY A

SOMETHING I WANT TO REMEMBER ABOUT TODAY

SOMETHING I COULD HAVE BEEN MORE GRATEFUL FOR TODAY

MY INTENTION FOR TOMORROW

Day 354

Day   Month   Year

Three things I'm grateful for

Something I want to remember about today   I give today a

My intention for   Something I could have been more grateful for today
tomorrow

DAY 355

DAY   MONTH   YEAR

THREE THINGS I'M GRATEFUL FOR

I GIVE TODAY A

SOMETHING I WANT TO REMEMBER ABOUT TODAY

SOMETHING I COULD HAVE BEEN MORE GRATEFUL FOR TODAY

MY INTENTION FOR
TOMORROW

DAY 356

Day   Month   Year

Three things I'm grateful for

Something I want to remember about today

I give today a

My intention for tomorrow

Something I could have been more grateful for today

DAY 357

DAY   MONTH   YEAR

THREE THINGS I'M GRATEFUL FOR

I GIVE TODAY A

SOMETHING I WANT TO REMEMBER ABOUT TODAY

SOMETHING I COULD HAVE BEEN MORE GRATEFUL FOR TODAY

MY INTENTION FOR TOMORROW

DAY 357

WEEK 51

THERE IS NO JOY WITHOUT GRATITUDE.

BRENÉ BROWN

SOMETHING I COULD HAVE BEEN MORE GRATEFUL FOR THIS WEEK

I GIVE THIS WEEK A

SOMETHING I WANT TO REMEMBER ABOUT THIS WEEK

MY INTENTION FOR NEXT WEEK

SOMEONE I COULD HAVE FELT MORE GRATEFUL FOR THIS WEEK

DAY 358

DAY   MONTH   YEAR

THREE THINGS I'M GRATEFUL FOR

I GIVE TODAY A

SOMETHING I WANT TO REMEMBER ABOUT TODAY

SOMETHING I COULD HAVE BEEN MORE GRATEFUL FOR TODAY

MY INTENTION FOR
TOMORROW

Day 359

Three things I'm grateful for

Something I want to remember about today   I give today a

My intention for   Something I could have been more grateful for today
tomorrow

DAY 360

Day   Month   Year

Three things I'm grateful for

I give today a

Something I want to remember about today

Something I could have been more grateful for today

My intention for tomorrow

DAY 361

DAY   MONTH   YEAR

THREE THINGS I'M GRATEFUL FOR

SOMETHING I WANT TO REMEMBER ABOUT TODAY

I GIVE TODAY A

MY INTENTION FOR
TOMORROW

SOMETHING I COULD HAVE BEEN MORE GRATEFUL FOR TODAY

DAY 362

DAY   MONTH   YEAR

THREE THINGS I'M GRATEFUL FOR

I GIVE TODAY A

SOMETHING I WANT TO REMEMBER ABOUT TODAY

SOMETHING I COULD HAVE BEEN MORE GRATEFUL FOR TODAY

MY INTENTION FOR TOMORROW

DAY 363

THREE THINGS I'M GRATEFUL FOR

SOMETHING I WANT TO REMEMBER ABOUT TODAY

I GIVE TODAY A

MY INTENTION FOR TOMORROW

SOMETHING I COULD HAVE BEEN MORE GRATEFUL FOR TODAY

DAY 364

DAY   MONTH   YEAR

THREE THINGS I'M GRATEFUL FOR

I GIVE TODAY A

SOMETHING I WANT TO REMEMBER ABOUT TODAY

SOMETHING I COULD HAVE BEEN MORE GRATEFUL FOR TODAY

MY INTENTION FOR TOMORROW

DAY 364

GRATITUDE WILL SHIFT YOU TO A HIGHER FREQUENCY, AND YOU WILL ATTRACT MUCH BETTER THINGS.

RHONDA BYRNE

SOMETHING I COULD HAVE BEEN MORE GRATEFUL FOR THESE PAST FOUR WEEKS

I GIVE THE PAST FOUR WEEKS A

SOMETHING I WANT TO REMEMBER ABOUT THE PAST FOUR WEEKS

MY INTENTION FOR THE NEXT FOUR WEEKS

SOMEONE I COULD HAVE FELT MORE GRATEFUL FOR THESE PAST FOUR WEEKS

DAY 365

THREE THINGS I'M GRATEFUL FOR

I GIVE TODAY A

SOMETHING I WANT TO REMEMBER ABOUT TODAY

SOMETHING I COULD HAVE BEEN MORE GRATEFUL FOR TODAY

MY INTENTION FOR TOMORROW

(DAY 366)

Day   Month   Year

Three things I'm grateful for

Something I want to remember about today

I give today a

My intention for tomorrow

Something I could have been more grateful for today

12 MONTHS

You've made it through a year of gratitude! Let's do a final check-in and see what the past three months have brought you.

SOMETHING I WANT TO REMEMBER ABOUT THE PAST THREE MONTHS

LOOKING BACK OVER THE PAST THREE MONTHS, I AM MOST GRATEFUL FOR

THE BIGGEST LESSON I LEARNED OVER THE PAST THREE MONTHS

SOMEONE OR SOMETHING I COULD HAVE FELT MORE GRATEFUL FOR DURING THE PAST THREE MONTHS

12 MONTHS

I GIVE THE PAST THREE MONTHS A

WHAT HAVE I BEEN UNABLE TO FEEL
GRATEFUL FOR DURING THE PAST THREE
MONTHS? CAN I REFORMULATE THAT
THOUGHT ANYWAY?

I AM GRATEFUL....

WHEN LOOKING BACK ON HOW I'VE RATED
MY WEEKS THUS FAR, THE NUMBERS TELL ME

MY INTENTION FOR THE NEXT THREE MONTHS

WHO HAVE I BEEN UNABLE TO FEEL GRATEFUL FOR DURING THE PAST THREE MONTHS? CAN I
REFORMULATE THAT THOUGHT ANYWAY? I AM GRATEFUL....

It goes without saying

that I would love to hear your story and how you got along.

If we aren't already in touch one way or the other, you can find me here:

MARIELLE@MSWORDSMITH.NL
MSWORDSMITH.NL
FACEBOOK.COM/MSWORDSMITH
INSTAGRAM.COM/MARIELLESSMITH

If you never want to miss an update about what I'm doing, you can sign up for my newsletter here:

MSWORDSMITH.NL/NEWSLETTER

I would also love for you to leave a review on Goodreads or where you purchased this book. Honest reviews are vital to our work being found and read.

Want More?

Gratitude is the wine for the soul. Go on. Get drunk.

Rumi

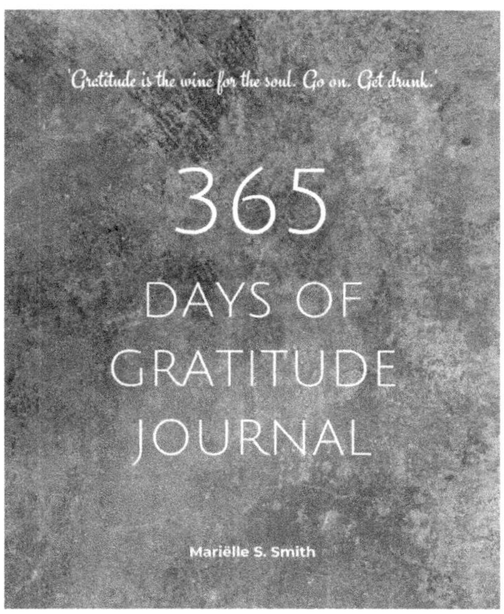

Go to mswordsmith.nl/365daysofgratitude and get the first volume of the *365 Days of Gratitude Journal*.

Already worked your way through Vol. 1? Sign up for my newsletter and be the first to hear when Vol. 3 is coming out!

Acknowledgements

I am immensely grateful that I have

a PARTNER who loves me unconditionally

a MOTHER to dedicate a work to

a BROTHER who roots for me

and

FRIENDS who see me
and believe in me more than I do